BBC REVIEW
of the
YEAR 1990

BBC REVIEW
of the
YEAR 1990

Edited by

Alex Gerlis *and* James Hogan

BBC BOOKS

Published by BBC Books,
a division of BBC Enterprises Limited,
Woodlands, 80 Wood Lane, London W12 0TT

First published November 1990
BBC REVIEW *of the* YEAR 1990 went to press on 25 October 1990

ISBN 0 563 36088 7

The editors and publisher would like to thank
Audience Selection, the Department of Employment, Gallup,
Goldman Sachs International Limited, Harris Research, ICM Research,
MORI and NOP Market Research Limited
for their assistance in compiling some of the
information used within this book.

Set in 10½/11 pt Baskerville by Ace Filmsetting Ltd, Frome
Printed and bound in England by Richard Clay Ltd, St Ives plc, Bungay
Cover printed by Richard Clay Ltd, St Ives plc, Norwich

Contents

FOREWORD 9

1 THE NEW DECADE 10
Alex Gerlis and James Hogan

2 UPHEAVALS – EUROPE AND THE GULF 22
John Simpson

3 BRITISH POLITICS –
THE PURSUIT OF POWER 36
John Cole

4 VOTING FOR POWER 50
Peter Snow

5 BRITAIN'S ECONOMY 64
Peter Jay

6 BRITAIN'S CHANGING SOCIETY 78
Polly Toynbee

7 AMERICA IN THE BUSH ERA 92
Gavin Esler

8 SOUTH AFRICA AT THE CROSSROADS 106
David Dimbleby

9 THE POLITICS OF ART 120
Andrew Burroughs

10 MEDIA REVOLUTION   134
Peter Fiddick

11 THE SPORTING YEAR   148
Archie Macpherson

12 FACING THE FUTURE   162
Peter Sissons

WHO DIED IN 1990   174

The editors

Alex Gerlis is a senior producer on BBC TV's *Breakfast News*. Since joining the BBC in 1983 he has worked on a wide range of news and current affairs programmes.

James Hogan also works in news and current affairs for the BBC, which he joined on leaving university. Currently editor of *Question Time*, he has previously worked on many other programmes including *Panorama* and *Newsnight*.

Kenneth Macintosh, the researcher of this book, is with BBC TV News Events.

The contributors

Andrew Burroughs is arts correspondent of BBC TV News and Current Affairs. He joined the BBC World Service in 1984 and moved to BBC TV News in 1986.

John Cole has been political editor of the BBC since 1981. He was previously deputy editor of *The Observer* and of *The Guardian*. He writes a weekly column on politics in *The Listener*.

David Dimbleby is a presenter of *Panorama* and of many special BBC TV current affairs programmes. He has covered South Africa extensively in 1990 for *Panorama*.

Gavin Esler is the chief North America correspondent of BBC TV News and Current Affairs. He was formerly a reporter and presenter on *Newsnight* and was also with the BBC in Northern Ireland.

Peter Fiddick, the editor of *The Listener*, is a contributor to a number of BBC programmes. He was previously media editor of *The Guardian*.

Peter Jay was appointed economics editor of the BBC in 1989. He has been with *The Times*, London Weekend Television and TV-am and has also been a Treasury civil servant and British ambassador to the USA.

Archie Macpherson, a sports reporter and presenter since 1963, has been the BBC's Scottish football correspondent and a sports presenter on BBC TV's *Breakfast News*.

John Simpson, who was appointed BBC foreign affairs editor in 1988, joined the BBC from university and has worked as a correspondent throughout the world for both radio and television.

Peter Sissons joined the BBC in 1989 as presenter of BBC TV's *Question Time* and *The Six O'Clock News*. He was previously presenter of ITN's *Channel Four News*.

Peter Snow has been a presenter of BBC TV's *Newsnight* since 1979 and is one of the presenters of the BBC *Election Specials*. He was previously with ITN.

Polly Toynbee has been social affairs editor of the BBC since 1988. Before joining the BBC she was a newspaper journalist for twenty years, with *The Observer* and with *The Guardian*.

Foreword

BBC Review of the Year 1990 is intended as an overview of the year, up to the time of going to press, rather than as an exhaustive checklist of every event in it. Each of the contributors has attempted to stand back from day-to-day events and instead highlight what they see as the broad themes that encapsulate the start of the new decade.

We would like to thank those people whose help and support made this project possible and who advised on different manuscripts. Needless to say, any faults or errors of judgment which remain are the responsibility of the editors.

We would especially like to pay tribute to Heather Holden-Brown, our commissioning editor at BBC Books, who has backed the project throughout. Also John Martin, Frank Phillips, Caroline Plaisted, Karen Willie, all at BBC Books. We would like to thank Tony Hall, the director of BBC News and Current Affairs, without whose support the project could not have been undertaken; the designer, David Robinson; the book's researcher, Kenneth Macintosh, whose excellent research skills enabled the book to be so wide-ranging; and Tricia Liddle and Sally Gray for the preparation and revision of the various manuscripts. Thanks are also due to Dr Peter Smith, who gave invaluable advice, and to our wives – Sonia Gerlis and Jane Hogan – for their patience throughout this project.

Most importantly, we would like to thank the authors of each of the chapters in the book – they have all kept to difficult deadlines in often demanding circumstances.

Alex Gerlis
James Hogan
London, October, 1990

The NEW DECADE

At the start of the last decade before

the new millennium, history changed

at an accelerating rate, culminating with

the once-antagonistic superpowers

taking a joint stand on the Gulf crisis

Alex Gerlis and James Hogan

B efitting the start of the last decade of the twentieth century, 1990 was a remarkable year. The historic changes witnessed in key parts of the world during 1989 continued into 1990 as new geopolitical formations took shape. The world experienced apocalyptic change: the wholescale collapse of Soviet-style communism; the reunification of Germany which had seemed remote or impossible until recently; and the gradual emergence of a new European order, embryonic for the past thirty years, but now apparently a concrete reality.

For the first six months of 1990 great change accompanied great optimism that the world was not simply undergoing a profound transformation but was also somehow entering an era of stillness and calm, where the threat of nuclear war and conflagration had been expunged, where the spirit of co-operation might at last prevail across different cultures and territorial boundaries.

Suddenly there seemed to be mounting evidence for this new global force, signs of change for the better. East–West confrontation now looked redundant, a thing of the past. The Warsaw Pact, under the weight of sheer necessity and in the wake of the first free elections in Eastern Europe since the start of the cold war, officially transformed itself into a somewhat looser organisation designed more for common security than expansionist aggression. The world was promised not only more peaceful times but a so-called 'peace dividend' that would allow governments to spend far less on defence and rectify hard-pressed budgets.

Elsewhere in the world, great and good causes also appeared to achieve a breakthrough. As *David Dimbleby* describes in his chapter, *South Africa at the Crossroads*, the South African president, F. W. de Klerk, turned his back on some of the most hateful aspects of apartheid and introduced reforms that would have been unthinkable, not to say unforgivable, inside his own party, even a year ago.

The release of Nelson Mandela, imprisoned for twenty-seven years for his opposition to South Africa's racialist policies and his support for the African National Congress, provided an existential moment in South African history that extended to the international community. The unbanning of the ANC and the continuing talks between Mr Mandela and the South African government, no matter how vexed or perilous, signalled a deep-seated change in one of the world's most tragic and tangled situations.

Yet, despite the speed of change and the ensuing optimism that went along with it, the year's events also drove home the harsh reality that the world is a rough and ready place, easily destabilised, most of all during periods of metamorphosis on a grand scale.

On 2 August Iraq, led by Saddam Hussein, invaded Kuwait. Iraq's action was almost universally condemned. It emphasised with brutal and startling simplicity that the world is an inherently dangerous place, especially when economic self-interest and semi-religious fervour are combined. Iraq's invasion of Kuwait was not only a major international crisis but also laid bare the false belief that we were entering a new age of certainty and consent.

For all the easing of East–West tension, therefore, an overview of the year's events produces a deeply ambivalent picture.

Throughout the year the no doubt brilliant but floundering Soviet leader Mikhail Gorbachev was plunged into a seemingly perpetual crisis that seemed ready to consume him at any time. He witnessed the formal break-up of the Soviet empire as one East European country after another not only rejected communist philosophy in the first free elections since the Forties, but did so in some cases by voting in favour of its polar opposite, conservative capitalism.*John Simpson,*

'I am going to visit all the countries in the world, eat all the food in the world, drink all the drink and make love, I hope, to all the women in the world, and maybe then get a good night's sleep.'
Brian Keenan on his release from captivity in Beirut

in *Upheavals – Europe and the Gulf*, analyses this process. The separatist crusade that has marched through Eastern Europe in the past twelve months now threatens the Soviet Union itself. The secessionist cause sprawls from the once downtrodden and terrified Baltic states of Latvia, Lithuania and Estonia to the citadel of Soviet eminence, Russia, led by Mr Gorbachev's great adversary, Boris Yeltsin. It is a measure of the Soviet Union's historic plight and growing plurality that Mr Yeltsin has been able to co-exist with Mr Gorbachev within the Soviet system while constantly denouncing and undermining the leader's right to govern.

Political chit chat – Mikhail Gorbachev and Boris Yeltsin at the Soviet Communist party congress.

The Soviet Union in 1990 thus presented a fearful spectacle that could so easily go tragically wrong. A once great power, with massive military might and a vast nuclear arsenal behind it, faces economic collapse and national humiliation. The risk of counter-reaction to what has already taken place, swinging violently towards either a new form of hard-headed Stalinism or semi-anarchy, is all too real. Mr Gorbachev's desperate attempts to steer a middle course by introducing semi-market-oriented change, even if it eventually works, has left the Soviet leader weakened with each attempt. Yet he, or his successors, have no alternative but to soldier on. By late September, Mr Gorbachev was reduced to ruling by decree. There is now, inside and outside the Soviet Union, open speculation about the survival of a Soviet leader and his policies.

But the collapse of communism in Europe should not mask the fact that it is still very much in power in China, a country that has been little in the news this year after the upheavals of 1989, although it contains one quarter of the world's population.

While the pace of change inside the Soviet bloc has been seismic, arguably the most powerful emergent force on the world stage has been the new Europe, itself partly a by-product of the disintegration of the Soviet empire. The newly enfranchised countries of Eastern Europe face a brighter but uncertain future. Newly liberated, they are confronted by a wide variety of problems ranging from the sociological to the broadly economic as they make the transition from state control to a free society. This process requires great adjustment, re-education and the courage to dispense with false subsidies.

None the less the potential power and influence of the former Soviet satellites, harnessed to a wider Europe, is very considerable. Collectively they constitute a huge market. The process of change inside these countries, already in a state of flux, has clearly fuelled the wider processes of change and closer co-operation in Europe as a whole. This dynamic was most dramatically demonstrated in the case of Germany. In 1990 the German people witnessed the spectacle of East Germany freely electing its own government in March, saw the reunification of Germany as a whole in October and planned all-German elections in December. Following a fierce debate between western governments and the Soviet Union, the new Germany will be a full member of both the European Community and NATO. Germany is thus poised to take a leading role in the emergence of a new European order which itself will arguably be bigger and more powerful than at any time this century.

The rise of nationalism in many parts of Eastern Europe, not least in the Soviet Union and the newly reunited Germany, has been a growing concern in 1990. The changing map of Europe and the potential influences of a reunited Germany was reflected in all European capitals. The European issue has been a wild card in British politics for well over a quarter of a century. And so it proved this year. The debate was dominated by two broad themes, worries about the overweening power of the new Germany and Britain's membership of the exchange rate mechanism.

'It would be unprecedented if at the end of the twentieth century one country could strangle another one while the whole world is watching.'
Kazimiera Prunskiene, prime minister of Lithuania

13

'Life and
society are
knocking on the
door of the
Communist
party and yet
this congress
does not hear
it. The tragedy
which is taking
place in our
country is not
being listened
to. The
leadership
simply does not
take it in.'
Boris Yeltsin,
president of the
Russian Federation

The argument inside Mrs Thatcher's cabinet over the summer about the make-up of the German people and the dangers of German reunification proved highly embarrassing. The fiercely populist, anti-European remarks made by the then secretary of state for trade and industry, Nicholas Ridley, in an article in *The Spectator*, were widely condemned by the political establishment in Britain and the rest of Europe. Mrs Thatcher, who had a few months earlier convened a special seminar on Germany, was reluctantly forced to accept Mr Ridley's grudging resignation.

As *Peter Jay* emphasises, in *Britain's Economy*, Britain's membership of the European monetary system and, in particular, the exchange rate mechanism, came to the boil this year. The issue became a matter of the utmost political significance for a government attempting to get the economy in shape for the next election. Mrs Thatcher's fears about monetary union are highly developed. She is concerned that being tied to other European currencies, notably the Deutschmark, will disadvantage the British economy. She is also suspicious of what she sees as the semi-socialist intentions of the so-called Delors plan, drawn up by Jacques Delors, EC president, which sets out a fast-track approach for European integration. Hence the prime minister's insistence that Britain should wait for inflation to fall before joining the ERM and the plan floated by her chancellor, John Major, for a hard ecu, instead of the Delors-inspired single European currency. Britain's gradualist approach gained support when the hard ecu, which allows individual countries to retain their own currencies, was unexpectedly endorsed in the autumn at a meeting of EC finance ministers.

The ERM proved a more intractable problem. Throughout the year there was endless speculation about the necessary conditions and timing of Britain's entry. The debate was sharpened by rising inflation, partly due to the Gulf crisis, and the proximity of the next election. Those people who believed in the so-called golden scenario ('join the ERM, interest rates and inflation fall, win the next election') argued the government should join over the summer. The fact that the prime minister's inflation target would not be met – inflation was actually rising and was nearly 11 per cent by the autumn – was irrelevant. The summer came and went without Britain joining the ERM. Britain's entry, just before the Conservative party conference, was taken as a pointer to a 1991 election.

The preoccupation with the state of the economy

in Britain during the year was partly a function of the marked downturn in the country's economic fortunes, and partly due to the electoral standing of the different political parties. There was a steady stream of bad economic news. Inflation continued to rise. Interest rates were obdurately high. Unemployment started to climb. Share prices fell steeply after Iraq invaded Kuwait. On top of this, various economic forecasts reported declining business confidence and falling order books. The CBI called it a recession.

As *Peter Snow* in *Voting for Power* observes, the deteriorating state of the economy offset any repeat of a Falklands effect in the opinion polls once the Gulf crisis started. Although the prime minister handled the situation personally, the polls remained fairly steadily in Labour's favour. As the government's counter-inflation policy is a medium-term strategy, the prime minister faces the prospect of fighting her first election in which the political and economic cycles may be out of kilter.

Against a weakening economic background the government endured a difficult, at times trying, year, especially for Mrs Thatcher. The May local elections threatened to be a disaster for the Conservatives. The poll tax, or community charge, came into force in England and Wales in 1990, with 38 million people being asked to pay it. Introducing new taxes is always a risky business, especially when millions of people are being asked to pay a local tax for the first time. In the event, the results of the elections were not nearly as bad as many Conservatives feared. Staunchly pro-Thatcherite councils like Wandsworth and Westminster were re-elected with increased majorities. Conservative party chairman Kenneth Baker claimed a famous victory, displaying a masterly command of his own public relations. The threat of a leadership challenge, possibly from a serious contender like Michael Heseltine, thus receded. But overall the results were bad for the Conservatives, good for Labour. Increasingly aware of the dangers that lay ahead, the government authorised substantial subsidies for local authorities next year to ease the burden of the poll tax. Whether this will be enough to make poll tax, which after all tackles the central issue of local government accountability, popular or at least less unpopular remains to be seen.

The housing market generally, so much a symbol of Mrs Thatcher's property-owning democracy, remained stagnant and depressed throughout the year. The high level of mortgage repayments pushed house prices down in real terms. Ominously – for the government – the number of repossessions reached record levels this year. In the first six months of 1990 they had doubled to over 14,000.

As *John Cole* observes in *The Pursuit of Power*, 1990 witnessed the return of two-party politics and a strong opposition. If Mrs Thatcher could no longer rely on good economic news to boost her standing, nor could she look to an unelectable opposition to make unforced errors. Labour spent the year consolidating the party's new programme around a modern mixed-market philosophy and moderate image. Throughout the spring Labour ran far ahead of the Conservatives in the

Margaret Thatcher inspects the Air Defense Operations Center at Cheyenne Mountain in Colorado.

polls with leads of up to 20 per cent. Proof that Labour could translate leads of this magnitude into actual results came in March when Sylvia Heal won the Mid-Staffordshire by-election by a landslide. Labour took the seat from the Conservatives with a 21 per cent swing, its best result since the 1930s.

No doubt aware of the danger of looking weak or unpatriotic, Labour carefully tracked the government's position on the Gulf crisis, only diverging from it where world opinion, as over the relative roles of the UN and USA, appeared to differ. Labour's handling of the Gulf – carefully constructed and united – was in marked contrast to the party's performance during the Falklands war at the start of the Eighties.

Similarly cautious and carefully targeted was Labour's economic message, spelt out over the summer. No doubt aware that it is not enough simply to attack the government over high interest rates and inflation, the Labour leadership unveiled its plans for a high growth, high consumption economy. This would have the double virtue of allowing the Labour party and the country to have its cake and eat it.

Interviewed by David Dimbleby, Neil Kinnock emphasised that a future Labour government would not significantly raise taxes. The majority of people, he

Labour leader Neil Kinnock in relaxed mood, with his party riding high in the polls.

said, would pay no extra taxes at all. He emphasised that increases in public spending would have to be funded out of increased productivity. The subsequent row over Mr Kinnock's figures, definitions of rich and poor, who may or may not pay more taxes, only served to remind people of the significance which will be attached to the economy in the run-up to the next election. For dedicated Labour watchers, however, the wrangle had unnerving overtones of the last election campaign when Labour came unstuck over the same issue.

Labour finally reaped the reward this year for the squeeze its shift to the right has put on the two centre parties. The final demise of Dr David Owen's Social Democrats was announced in early summer following disastrous performances in the Bootle by-election, where they polled fewer votes than the Monster Raving Loony party, and the local elections in May where they held on to just a handful of seats.

The Liberal Democrats also suffered from the squeeze on the minor parties. Their opinion poll rating throughout most of the year was stuck around 9 per cent, but they polled significantly better in the local elections with some 18 per cent of the vote. The Greens, who were a promising new electoral force just a year ago, saw their electoral support wane in 1990.

Twenty years after the troubles began in Northern Ireland a solution seemed no nearer. The attempts by the secretary of state for Northern Ireland, Peter Brooke, to advance the spirit of co-operation between Catholics and Protestants within the framework of the Anglo-Irish agreement was marred by the brutal, senseless killing of Ian Gow, the prime minister's friend and colleague. Mr Brooke's manoeuvres to break the deadlock in Ulster were as tortuous as they were laudable. When Sir Peter Terry, the man who was governor of Gibraltar at the time of the SAS shootings, was shot at his home near Stafford in September it was the seventeenth IRA attack in Britain itself in 1990 – the highest number of such incidents since 1974. Even the prime minister commented that the IRA was fighting a guerrilla war.

Closer to home, the government's reforming zeal where the National Health Service is concerned, as *Polly Toynbee* observes in *Britain's Changing Society*, represents a real electoral risk. The government has pressed on with its radical overhaul of NHS practices, despite staunch opposition, throughout the year. If its plans work it will no doubt eventually be applauded. However, in the short run, the danger is that patients will feel that

'These murders are as odious as they are futile. Once again, wives have been turned into widows and children into orphans and for what purpose? There is a terrifyingly perverted purposelessness in this attack, as in all IRA attacks. But there is one message that should go out. First, of sympathy to the families of those who have been murdered, and, secondly, a message to the IRA, that they will never, never win.'
Ian Gow speaking one week before his death from an IRA car bomb

standards have fallen and that a still much-valued institution has been needlessly undermined.

One area that will arguably be most affected by a deterioration in the economic situation is the deregulation of the air waves, intended to create a far more competitive media industry, as *Peter Fiddick* observes in *Media Revolution*. There will be many more terrestrial, satellite and cable television channels. These channels, which represent major capital investments, will be launched in inauspicious times. Advertising revenues fell steeply this year and are likely to go on doing so for some time. The tendering process whereby people will bid for different channels – as set out in the government's broadcasting bill – is likely to take place in a very difficult climate.

Nineteen ninety was also an eventful year for sport. *Archie Macpherson* writes on the year's sporting events and the political influences upon them in *The Sporting Year*. *Andrew Burroughs* in *The Politics of Art* covers the importance of outside influences in the world of art.

A year that started with the USA taking a back seat entered its later phase with the focus of attention very much on America's president, heralding *America in the Bush Era* as described by *Gavin Esler*. The Bush presidency enjoyed an extended honeymoon for the first year or so of its life. The only major embarrassment was Mr Bush's revelation half-way through the year that he might be forced to put up taxes, breaking his solemn promise to the American people. 'Read my lips,' he had implored throughout the presidential campaign that swept him to office, 'no new taxes.' Bush's attempts to tackle government spending later created an embarrassing crisis over the US budget.

It was, inevitably, the Gulf that was to pose the biggest test of the Bush presidency. The Gulf crisis provided the American people with an issue they could readily understand – goodies versus baddies. As such it has strengthened America's own perception of its role in the world.

The Gulf crisis also provided the USA and the USSR with the opportunity to put to the test their new-found relationship, an opportunity to show that the new world order was more than rhetoric. The US secretary of state called the Iraqi invasion of Kuwait, 'one of the defining moments of a new era', and the co-operation between the two great superpowers over the Gulf crisis showed that there was indeed substance to the remarkable changes that the world was now seeing.

The long-term issues likely to confront the world beyond this year are analysed in *Peter Sissons'* chapter,

'I am not trying to characterise threats. A threat is a vicious aggression against Kuwait and that speaks for itself. Anything collaterally is just simply more indication that these are outlaws, international outlaws and renegades . . . I will not discuss with you what my options are or might be, but they are wide open . . . Just wait, watch and learn.'
President Bush after the invasion of Kuwait in August

19

Driving a
straight course
– George Bush
on a 'business
as usual'
holiday in
Kennebunkport.

Facing the Future. Nineteen ninety lived up to the promise of the start of the last decade of the twentieth century. It was a year of spectacular change in which hope and fear, opportunity and danger, were not only inextricably mixed but ever present. Journalism, it is said, is the first draft of history and 1990 was one of those years in which we were acutely aware throughout the year that we were watching history in the making. *BBC Review of the Year 1990* is intended to reflect that process.

Upheavals ~ EUROPE and the GULF

As the dust cleared from the revolutions

in Eastern Europe, and the world

looked towards peace between America

and the Soviet Union, a new spectre arose

in the Gulf

John Simpson

As late as October a year ago no one was suggesting that 1989 might be compared with 1789, 1848 and 1917 as one of the great revolutionary moments. And yet, within a matter of weeks, the Soviet empire in Europe had collapsed, and Poland, Hungary, the German Democratic Republic, Czechoslovakia and Romania had effectively ceased to be Marxist-Leninist states. The Cold War was declared officially over. A new era of peace and co-operation seemed about to start. One historian, more reckless than most, declared that since there was only one political philosophy – liberal democracy – left alive in the world, history was dead. Even those who thought that was foolish believed that the world was better shielded from conflict than at any time since the middle of the nineteenth century. Others went further back, recalling the famous judgment in *The Decline and Fall of the Roman Empire*. 'The world', wrote one historian-journalist at the beginning of 1990, 'is probably a safer place now than at any time since the period of which Gibbon wrote with such enthusiasm: that which elapsed from the death of Domitian to the accession of Commodus.'

But events move faster nowadays than they have at

any time in history. Six months after that was written, Iraq invaded Kuwait. The possibility of a major war, involving chemical and even nuclear weapons, erupted. The comfortable talk of peace, the hopes for a new world order, were forgotten. The change in atmosphere was comparable to an armed robbery interrupting a wedding reception. At the time of writing, the outcome of the crisis in the Gulf is as impossible to judge as the original invasion was unexpected. History has not died; what has died is the fatuous notion that because Marxism-Leninism has collapsed as a serious challenger to liberal democracy, there are no other alternatives. The conflict in the Gulf has shown that third world resentment, Arab nationalism and Islamic fundamentalism are every bit as hostile to self-satisfied, unthinking, western interests as Soviet communism was. The brave new world order which seemed to have begun at the summit in December 1989, when President Bush met President Gorbachev on board a Soviet naval ship in the choppy waters of an obscure Maltese harbour, had lasted unchallenged for little more than eight months.

Nevertheless, there have been clear and irreversible changes in the world in 1990, which neither the Gulf crisis nor anything else can affect. The ending of the cold war has changed attitudes and relationships throughout the entire world this year. In Cambodia, in Afghanistan, in South Africa, in Central Europe, in Central America, even in the Middle East, the two countries which we used to call the superpowers have begun to make something like a common cause. And because they understand each other better, and are looking for a co-operative rather than a competitive relationship, there is hope of improvement in each of these areas. The release of Nelson Mandela and the dismantling of apartheid could not have taken place if the South African government had been afraid of Soviet intervention. Instead, Moscow has given the process its blessing. Until the invasion of Kuwait changed everything, it seemed reasonable to hope that something roughly similar might happen over the Palestinian question and the West Bank.

Since the Soviet Union has ceased to identify its strategic interests as being the opposite of those of the United States, and vice versa, areas of turbulence and confrontation no longer need to involve the global balance or ideology. In the 1970s, when the international competition between the superpowers was at its height and each was hunting for clients in the third world, it took very little to create an atmosphere of crisis. The events of 1990 have changed all that. But chief among those events, more important than anything except a bad outcome from the Gulf crisis, has been the internal collapse of the Soviet Union.

In 1990, the accelerating social and economic collapse within the Soviet Union made it more necessary than ever for the men at the top of the system – and particularly for Mr Gorbachev and Mr Shevardnadze – to maintain reasonable relations with the West. Competition along the old lines is simply impossible: it would be too expensive, and it would block the way to the loans and credits from the United States and Western Europe

War and peace – US aircraft carrier *Saratoga* passing through the city of Suez on its way to the Gulf.

which are probably the sole chance of survival for the Soviet Union if it is to remain a unitary state. There are clear indications that people lower down the Soviet system, particularly in the military leadership, do not accept that the Soviet Union is as weak as its top leaders insist. Even senior generals complained in public about the lack of support Moscow was offering to Iraq after the years in which the Iraqis had come to rely on Soviet weaponry, and there was anger that the United States should have established its forces in Saudi Arabia, relatively close to the Soviet Union's sensitive southern flank.

Nevertheless, while western military analysts were

nervous at such outspoken criticism of the official Kremlin line, the fact remains that in the Soviet Union generals, like everyone else, are freer to say what they think now than at any time since the early 1920s. We have become used to the idea that because something is said publicly, it has a particular meaning and significance within the Soviet system. But the new freedom of expression means that a general's opinions do not necessarily have any more validity or force than those of a journalist, a factory manager or a local party boss. The higher up the system you go, the more certain people are that there has to be an accommodation with the West. The only threat to that consensus would come from some major upheaval which would destroy the present leadership of the Communist party entirely. There is an inevitable degree of loose talk within the Soviet system about coups and revolutions, but even if such a thing were to take place, the assumption is that it would merely render the Soviet Union less likely, rather than more likely, to be able to compete with the West on equal terms. Mikhail Gorbachev and Eduard Shevardnadze have not decided on the basis of some noble self-denying principle to end the Soviet Union's efforts to establish the Marxist-Leninist system in the rest of the world; it has become painfully obvious to them that the system cannot be made to function properly. That is an objective assessment which cannot be changed by the arrival of a new group in the Kremlin.

It is too early, in the autumn of 1990, to be able to say that the Soviet Union has finally ceased to matter in international affairs; with the biggest and most effective army, air force and navy still in place it cannot yet be ignored. But the will to carry on has evaporated. The Soviet Union is like a strong man who has forced himself to carry an immensely heavy burden too long. Its history over the past forty-five years has been one of extraordinary determination and self-discipline under the most difficult circumstances, but the effort has suddenly become too great to continue. The muscles and sinews are overstretched, the heart seriously strained. The Soviet Union is a hospital case, and will probably not leave the intensive care unit in its present form.

It was the realisation that the Soviet Union would not intervene to save the old leaders which led people in East Germany, Czechoslovakia, Romania and Bulgaria to come out into the streets in large numbers and challenge the ruling party which had been imposed on them for more than forty years. And yet, as 1990 drew on, there began to be serious doubts in each of the Eastern European states which had gone through a revolutionary phase at the end of 1989 about the genuine nature of the revolution. In Czechoslovakia, a government-established commission of inquiry discovered evidence which seemed to show that the KGB and its Czechoslovak counterpart, the StB, had deliberately fomented the demonstrations which led to the downfall of the old leadership.

In Romania, Silviu Brucan and other senior members of the National Salvation Front which took over when President Ceausescu was overthrown revealed that the Front had been in existence for some time before the supposed revolution, and that its assumption of power had been more in the nature of a coup than a spontaneous uprising. Brucan and his disaffected colleagues suggested that the Soviet Union had been behind the whole affair. There were similar doubts about the nature of the events of November 1989 in East Berlin, when the Wall was opened, and about the collapse of the hardliners in Bulgaria.

In each case – Czechoslovakia, Romania, East Germany and Bulgaria – it seemed possible to distinguish a pattern of sorts: the old guard, uniformly hostile to the new principles of reform which had become established in Moscow, were eased out. Reform-minded communists, sympathetic to the changes in the Soviet system, came to the forefront. In Romania and Bulgaria the plan – assuming it really existed – was remarkably successful, if only in the short run. In East Germany and Czechoslovakia it placed new men in power (Lothar de Maiziere and Vaclav Havel respectively) who had no interest in maintaining close or even particularly friendly relations with Moscow.

There is a wealth of circumstantial and other evidence to support the theory, even though at the time of writing it remains just that: a theory. Nevertheless, the mere suggestion that the revolutions of 1989 might have been engineered by the very country which most of the revolutionaries believed they were rejecting has a certain suitability to it. Even at the time, standing in Wenceslas Square, or at the Brandenburg Gate, or in front of the Central Committee building in Bucharest, it was obvious to many of us that this would be the best and happiest moment of the revolution; that whatever happened afterwards would inevitably be more disturbing, less uplifting, less altruistic. In each case, even that of Czechoslovakia, which always seemed most likely to do well from the greater freedom which the revolution brought, the aftermath has been one of gloom about the political future and anxiety about the possibility of economic collapse.

'I always knew we would be free. Otherwise I would not have gone to prison. But I am not the only one who has suffered, and I am not the only one who can lead our people.'
Vaclav Havel, president of Czechoslovakia

Man of the people – Czechoslovak president Vaclav Havel does a quick two-step in Southern Moravia.

At the beginning of 1990 things seemed rather different. Here was a sense of new possibilities, new hopes. It was reasonable to suppose that the United States and the European Community would soon begin rewarding the countries of Central and Eastern Europe which had broken away from Soviet influence. There were suggestions from politicians in Britain, the Netherlands and West Germany that room should be found for the new democracies in the ranks of the EC: if not immediately, then early in the next century. 'We cannot ignore these people,' said a leading German Social Democrat, 'they have deserved better of us than that.'

Others in the Community saw the sudden arrival of so many poor claimants on the European doorstep as a threat to the carefully prepared plans for 1992. At a meeting of the twelve permanent representatives in Brussels in January there were distinct signs of nervousness. 'The cake is only so big,' one was quoted as having said afterwards. 'If we have to cut extra pieces of it none of us is going to be happy.' Yet Margaret Thatcher and some of her ministers were pleased at the thought that a tightly unified Community of twelve could suddenly be presented as both a political anachronism and a selfish, inward-looking club for the rich and the moderately well-to-do. In 1990, European union ceased to look quite so good an answer to the problems of international division as it had appeared for more than thirty years.

That helped the doubters in other ways. Mrs Thatcher, having fought an increasingly unsuccessful rearguard action against the proposals put forward in 1989 by EC President Jacques Delors and the European Commission for economic and monetary union, found that the events in Eastern Europe had given her an unexpected degree of support. What had seemed to many, even in her own government, like instinctive little-Englandism, now took on the appearance of prudent statesmanship. As the year progressed, the poorer countries of the Community – Spain and Portugal in particular – came to share Britain's nervousness that full monetary union, with one central bank and a single currency, would work against the interests of the less successful.

By late summer, the original scope of the Delors plan had been seriously curtailed. Only a year before, the movement towards European union had seemed unstoppable, and countries and trading blocs throughout the world were beginning to come to terms with the idea of a Europe which would be, once again, at the centre of the international economy and international politics. The collapse of the Soviet empire in Eastern Europe changed everything. In particular it altered the perceptions of the EC's leading economy – the real engine of Western European integration. Now there was a new item at the top of the German agenda.

The call for a united Germany had always been a muted one in the Federal Republic. Almost everyone, even on the left of the SPD, agreed on the fundamental principle; and yet it had always had a slightly unclean feel to it. Too many of the wrong kind of people wanted it too much. So it was easier for most politicians to forget about it. Chancellor Helmut Kohl was not one of them. For personal as well as political reasons (his wife had been born in what became East Germany and joined the diaspora at the end of the Second World War) he held on to the idea with characteristic stubbornness. Even when the SPD seemed to have demonstrated conclusively that the way forward lay in reaching a better understanding with the East German regime, Dr Kohl and those in the CDU and CSU who thought like him continued to believe in the reality of a united Germany.

No one, however, expected that it would happen quite as it did. The sudden weakening of the power of the East German state in the summer of 1989 and its virtual collapse in November, when the Wall was

West German chancellor Helmut Kohl at the Brandenburg Gate.

breached, demonstrated the complete phoniness of a regime whose only strength had been the willingness of the Soviet Union to defend it at all costs. As the election of 18 March 1990 in East Germany approached, the moderate, reformed Communists united with the left wing of the newly active SPD in the East to campaign for some form of association between the two parts of Germany which would not amount to outright reunification. Their argument was that East Germany was too weak economically, and would be overwhelmed by West Germany's strength. But the voters had seized on the idea, carefully fostered by the Eastern Christian Democrats, that a vote for the CDU would not simply lead to German unity but also to a sharing of West German wealth. A country which had grown up in envy and self-denigration in the shadow of the Federal Republic was swept by dreams of getting rich quick. The Christian Democrats won the election handsomely, and Chancellor Kohl, with an eye on the elections at the end of 1990, pressed on quickly towards reunification.

'Probably I will not live to see it.'

West German chancellor Helmut Kohl speaking in 1988 about reunification of the two Germanies

The process was bound to be a humiliating one for the poor relations. Officers in the East German army found themselves selling their long-service medals to the stallholders at Checkpoint Charlie in order to buy half a kilo of decent coffee. Soon – much too soon for the financial health and self-respect of the East – West German companies began moving into the morass of the old GDR economy, taking over factories which had never been properly equipped, and whose workers had never done a proper day's work. At the plant which produced Trabant cars, the symbol of the East German flight to the West, a foreman said that nothing had changed in thirty years: the machinery, the style, the work practices, the pay.

One leading West German banker estimated the cost of bringing the East up to the environmental standards of the West at tens of billions of Deutschmarks. There was a souring of the public mood in the big cities of the Federal Republic as the cost of looking after so many economic refugees grew. By the middle of 1990, it had started to become painfully clear that a united Germany, far from threatening the stability of Europe and dominating the economies of its trading partners, would be saddled with a burden which would take years to cope with. In its collapse, the Soviet empire was taking its revenge on the system which had conquered it.

It also took its revenge on the nations which broke away from its control with such enthusiasm. In Czechoslovakia, whose revolution had been entirely peaceful, the recognition quickly grew that it had entered its new democratic phase seriously damaged by its experience of communism. Before the second world war, Czechoslovakia had been at least as rich and productive as its western neighbours; after forty-two years of enforced Marxism-Leninism its gross domestic product was little more than 40 per cent of West Germany's. Its emissions of sulphur dioxide exceeded 18 tonnes per square kilometre: the second worst figure in the entire world. In West Germany, by contrast, emissions amounted to 9 tonnes per sq km. A third of Czechoslovakia's forests and agricultural lands were seriously damaged. Infant mortality, alcoholism, and the number of people serving prison sentences were all far higher than in Western Europe. The coalition of Civic Forum and Public Against Violence which won the election of 9 June 1990 with 46.6 per cent of the vote in the House of the People had inherited a bitter legacy.

In Romania, everything had been harder for years. The dictatorship of Nicolae Ceausescu had damaged living standards, educational levels, and normal social relationships for three decades. The revolution of December 1989 was violent, and its outcome questionable. Opposition quickly arose to the National Salvation Front of Ion Iliescu, on the grounds that it was little more than a reformed Communist party. In the run-up to the elections of 20 May 1990 there were serious allegations from the Peasants' party and others that the Front was using a variety of unacceptable means to ensure its own victory. Most foreign observers accepted the result, which gave the Front 85.97 per cent of the vote, though not entirely without reservation. But it was not long before the demonstrators who occupied the main street of Bucharest in protest at the Front's unreconstructed approach were removed with considerable brutality by pro-government activists drafted in from the mines near Bucharest. Such legitimacy as the Front had obtained in the election quickly evaporated. Romania in 1990 had become almost as much of an embarrassment to the outside world as it had been before the revolution.

Poland's movement away from Soviet Marxism-Leninism and towards parliamentary democracy has been uncharacteristically gradual and quiet. The benefits have therefore been rather greater than for most of its neighbours. Even so, the process has not been an entirely easy one in 1990. After ten years, Solidarity, the coalition between intellectuals and workers, has begun to fall apart. The government of Tadeusz Mazowiecki, elected in 1989, had come under heavy criticism for

'In Leipzig, 350,000 people had come to hear Helmut Kohl. I will not see such a thing again. It is something which will not happen again. In Leipzig and Dresden they are as German as I am. Now they are saying it.'
West German chancellor Helmut Kohl speaking in 1990

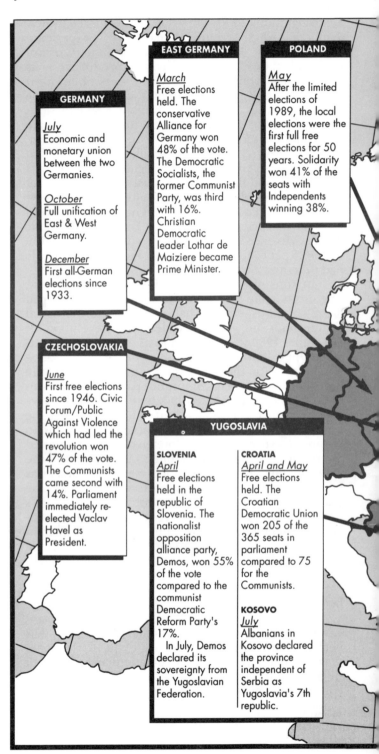

The 'NEW EUROPE' of 1990.

GERMANY

July
Economic and monetary union between the two Germanies.

October
Full unification of East & West Germany.

December
First all-German elections since 1933.

EAST GERMANY

March
Free elections held. The conservative Alliance for Germany won 48% of the vote. The Democratic Socialists, the former Communist Party, was third with 16%. Christian Democratic leader Lothar de Maiziere became Prime Minister.

POLAND

May
After the limited elections of 1989, the local elections were the first full free elections for 50 years. Solidarity won 41% of the seats with Independents winning 38%.

CZECHOSLOVAKIA

June
First free elections since 1946. Civic Forum/Public Against Violence which had led the revolution won 47% of the vote. The Communists came second with 14%. Parliament immediately re-elected Vaclav Havel as President.

YUGOSLAVIA

SLOVENIA
April
Free elections held in the republic of Slovenia. The nationalist opposition alliance party, Demos, won 55% of the vote compared to the communist Democratic Reform Party's 17%.
 In July, Demos declared its sovereignty from the Yugoslavian Federation.

CROATIA
April and May
Free elections held. The Croatian Democratic Union won 205 of the 365 seats in parliament compared to 75 for the Communists.

KOSOVO
July
Albanians in Kosovo declared the province independent of Serbia as Yugoslavia's 7th republic.

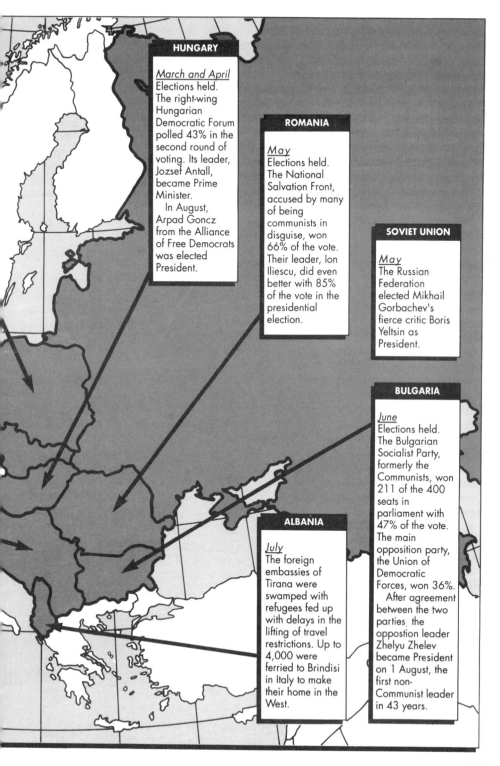

HUNGARY

March and April
Elections held.
The right-wing
Hungarian
Democratic Forum
polled 43% in the
second round of
voting. Its leader,
Jozsef Antall,
became Prime
Minister.

In August,
Arpad Goncz
from the Alliance
of Free Democrats
was elected
President.

ROMANIA

May
Elections held.
The National
Salvation Front,
accused by many
of being
communists in
disguise, won
66% of the vote.
Their leader, Ion
Iliescu, did even
better with 85%
of the vote in the
presidential
election.

SOVIET UNION

May
The Russian
Federation
elected Mikhail
Gorbachev's
fierce critic Boris
Yeltsin as
President.

BULGARIA

June
Elections held.
The Bulgarian
Socialist Party,
formerly the
Communists, won
211 of the 400
seats in
parliament with
47% of the vote.
The main
opposition party,
the Union of
Democratic
Forces, won 36%.

After agreement
between the two
parties, the
opposition leader
Zhelyu Zhelev
became President
on 1 August, the
first non-
Communist leader
in 43 years.

ALBANIA

July
The foreign
embassies of
Tirana were
swamped with
refugees fed up
with delays in the
lifting of travel
restrictions. Up to
4,000 were
ferried to Brindisi
in Italy to make
their home in the
West.

'Are you getting your milk Stuart? And your cornflakes, too? I do not think all Iraqi kids can get cornflakes now. So please forgive us, because we, like you, have our own children, like Stuart and like Ian . . . And we hope that you, as guests, your presence as guests here is not going to be for long, for too long. We want you to be safe and to go back to your countries, and this is not meant to be a propaganda scoop. I am not speaking for propaganda purposes, but it is truly a humanitarian concern that we want you to be safe.'

President Saddam Hussein with British families held in Baghdad

failing to deal once and for all with the old communist system, and during 1990 its efforts in this regard slowly gathered pace. Former opposition figures such as Janusz Onyszkiewicz and Krzysztof Kozlowski were put in position as deputy ministers in the defence and interior ministries to speed up the dismantling of the old Communist structure. General Jaruzelski, who introduced martial law in Poland in 1981 and lingered on as president ever since, is thought to have offered his resignation in January 1990; but increasing disagreements between the leading figures of what had once been Solidarity meant that for most of the year the question of the country's constitutional leadership was unsettled. Lech Walesa became an increasingly conservative figure, and some of his former colleagues, including Mazowiecki, considered standing for the presidency in order to ensure that Walesa would not be elected.

Of all the countries which had formerly been part of the Soviet bloc, only Hungary's path towards parliamentary democracy and economic liberalism was entirely smooth in 1990. There had been no sudden hitches and no abrupt revolutions such as each of the other former satellites had experienced in their different ways. The result was a satisfactory, if complicated election, in which the Hungarian Democratic Forum, the MDF, scored a convincing victory. Indeed, the 60 per cent which it and its potential coalition partners achieved was roughly equal to the share of the vote which the centre-right Smallholders' party won in 1945. In other words, Hungary seemed at last to be back on the rails, after the savage experiences of forty-five years of Soviet domination.

For a brief time in 1990, there was a good deal of talk in most western countries of the peace dividend which would accrue now that the cold war was deemed to be over. Major savings seemed possible in defence spending, and a new period of genuine co-operation seemed about to begin. Saddam Hussein of Iraq quickly ended that on 2 August 1990. Nevertheless, although any hope of a peace dividend for the United States and several of its allies was soon swallowed up by the cost of maintaining a powerful force in the Gulf, the new relationship between the superpowers took the strain of the crisis. The summit in Helsinki between President Bush and President Gorbachev showed that both men were committed to the concept of a new world order, in which the great military powers would endorse a peaceful solution to international problems. The overwhelming support of the United Nations

Iraqi TV Taped Broadcast

Security Council for resolutions 660 and 661, calling on Iraq to withdraw from Kuwait and laying down sanctions against it until the withdrawal took place, was another indication that a new world order was a serious possibility. At the time of writing the resolution of the Gulf crisis is far from clear, and an outcome is conceivable in which, even in defeat, Saddam Hussein might be able to arouse powerful feelings in the Islamic world against the West. But even if that were to happen, there has been an unprecedented movement towards international agreement. For all the disappointments during the year in Europe, East and West, that will be the longest-lasting and most significant outcome of 1990.

Iraqi President Saddam Hussein pats the head of a young western hostage in a sickly publicity stunt.

35

British Politics ~ the PURSUIT of POWER

Europe was a problem, the centre

parties crumbled and Labour took the

lead in the polls.

Mrs Thatcher wobbled on her pedestal

– but she did not falter

John Cole

Nineteen ninety has been the year when the political earth moved. For a decade, Margaret Thatcher had ruled without serious electoral challenge. It is true that between elections, especially before the Falklands War in 1982, and after the Westland crisis in 1986, she looked personally vulnerable. And there was a period in the early Eighties when a man on a galloping horse – had he stopped to read the opinion polls – might have concluded that the Alliance was poised, not only to defeat Mrs Thatcher, but to sweep both older parties from their long supremacy. But these proved to be brief intermissions of political excitement, which evaporated when the general elections of 1983 and 1987 were called. Both produced Tory landslides.

The Prime Minister had looked more vulnerable in the spring of 1990 than ever before. Her endeavours, in May 1989, to circumvent celebration and evaluation of her first decade in power have proved yet again what a strong sense of political self-preservation she has. For the media celebration did, indeed, damage her: drawing attention to the passage of time; making her as much a target for her opponents as a totem for her supporters; and – following the old Westminster dictum that opponents are on the opposite side of the House, but enemies all around you – it re-ignited the ambitions of Tory aspirants to succeed her.

We were not far into 1990 before the Conservatives' previous appearance of impregnability had been badly dented. The economy had gone awry, and inflation, interest rates and mortgages were all at levels which kept the government unpopular. By the autumn, with inflation in double figures and unemployment on a rising trend again, opponents were asking what was left of the Thatcher economic miracle. The

Margaret Thatcher pictured in the early Eighties with close friend Ian Gow, murdered by the IRA in July.

Conservative answer was that British industry had been transformed, and that a new efficiency would bring benefits in the longer-term.

Labour's poll lead, which had been hovering in high single figures during the second half of 1989, set firmly in double figures during the first half of 1990. For a time in the spring, it moved towards, and even above, twenty points, inducing near-panic among Conservative MPs with small, or even moderate majorities.

What had brought about this remarkable change? The themes of 1990 originate towards the end of the previous year. Sir Anthony Meyer's token challenge for the Conservative leadership may have produced only sixty MPs who either voted for him or abstained. But I subsequently learned that George Younger and his team of Thatcher helpers had found it difficult to persuade a further forty or fifty Tories to submerge their doubts. She was, for a time, on probation.

An even more damaging fissure, which had opened in Conservative unity in 1989, became a running sore during 1990. This was the issue over which Nigel Lawson had resigned as chancellor: British entry into the European exchange rate mechanism. By the middle of 1990, when Lawson and his arch-enemy, Sir Alan Walters, the prime minister's economic adviser, had long since left the corridors of power, we were still being assured that Sir Alan's continuing visits to Downing Street merely revealed him as a 'friend of the family'.

Seasoned observers found it hard to believe that Denis Thatcher likes nothing better, after *Rugby Special* on a Sunday afternoon, than a cosy chat with Walters about the ERM. But pause a moment: this may not be the jolliest form of pastime the prime minister's husband can imagine; however Mr Thatcher does believe that his wife's Bruges speech, in which she raised her Euro-sceptic flag at the heart of British politics, will be judged by historians as among her most significant contributions to public affairs.

So the quarrel over Europe that burst into the headlines with the Lawson and Walters resignations is no mere breakdown in personal relations. It went to the heart of a debate which could split a party as readily as the Corn Laws did in the last century. The bitter arguments over British membership of the European Community in the Sixties, which appeared to have been settled by the referendum of 1975, have broken out in a different, more complicated, but scarcely less visceral form. Now they are about the renewed drive, originating in Bonn, Paris, and Brussels, to create a closer economic, and ultimately political, union.

Mrs Thatcher finds European political manoeuvring uncongenial. Colleagues maintain that the turbulent events of 1990 – failures in the economy, the poll tax row, her own unprecedented unpopularity in the polls – have left her, if not chastened, then less dogmatic in discussion, more inclined to take her decisions pragmatically. Yet she slips back into her old style sometimes, especially over Europe.

One minister chuckles about a July cabinet, when John Major reported on French and German ideas about economic help to the Soviet Union. The prime minister went into rhetorical overdrive and, abandoning her more conciliatory tones, laid down the law in a way even she probably recognised went a bit over the top. The chancellor waited till she had finished, and then said: 'I am deeply grateful to you, prime minister, for giving me that gentle steer.' The meeting dissolved in laughter, and John Major had won some freedom to manoeuvre.

Europe is potential dynamite for both big political parties. The Liberal Democrats, because their commitment to the Community is of much longer standing, escape disputes. Labour, in opposition, has been able to skate over disagreements. Neil Kinnock has made one of his most significant transformations in policy, leaving his party sounding much more enthusiastic than the government about some, at least, of the proposals of the president of the European Commission, Jacques Delors, for economic and monetary union. True, there have been rumblings from influential Labour anti-Europeans, like Peter Shore and Michael Foot, but this is nothing like as acute a problem for an opposition party as for a government.

For enthusiastic Tory Europeans, the worry was that the prime minister's delay in accepting even the first stage of the Delors plan had left Britain as the last Community country to join the ERM. Britain's path to that nirvana – if so it proves – has lain over mangled political bodies on both sides of the argument. If, on the pro-entry side, Sir Geoffrey Howe was maimed and Nigel Lawson killed by disputes with the prime minister, on the sceptical wing of the cabinet, Nicholas Ridley has also thrown himself on the barbed wire. Yet, over the corpses, the new men, Douglas Hurd and John Major, managed to achieve Britain's entry into the ERM on the eve of the Tory conference.

Those British Conservatives who are reluctant to surrender any new powers to Europe act principally on

free-market principles, though the spectre of lost parliamentary sovereignty is also prayed in aid. Economic
sovereignty might some day become an issue for a
Labour government also, since freedom to devalue has
been a weapon that some Labour people – by no means
all on the left of the party – traditionally cherish.

So why did Labour nail its colours to the ERM
masthead? One reason is obvious: because international finance is hostile to its policies, the advent of a
Labour government is often accompanied by a sterling
crisis. Membership of the ERM should ease that. The
less discussed reason centres on one of the sleeping

**Chancellor of
the exchequer
John Major tries
to fight off
inflation and
recession.**

dilemmas of British politics, to which neither major party has found an answer: wage inflation. Because the present bout of inflation did not begin with wages and salaries, public comment has skirted round this endemic British problem: that from boardroom to workbench, we tend to pay ourselves for more than we produce.

The collapse of incomes policy in the dying months of the Callaghan government a decade ago has so disillusioned the present Labour leadership that it has avoided discussing any form of incomes policy. But the ERM requires sterling to remain within a band in relation to other European currencies. Would John Smith, as Labour chancellor, not have a good reason for telling the unions they must choose between an expanded economy and desirable public spending, on the one hand, and a totally free market in wages and salaries, on the other? There were some signs towards the end of 1990 that both unions and the shadow cabinet were thinking more about wages. In Mrs Thatcher's brand of Conservatism, only exhortation to wage-bargainers is permissible, and ministers were hard at that throughout the year.

Europe and the economy were the deep-seated issues of 1990 politics, but what has made most sparks fly at Westminster is the poll tax. This offered the chance for a good, old-fashioned battle between government and opposition, which voters found more comprehensible than the complexities of the European Monetary System. The debate within the Conservative party on how to reform local government finance has been going on for 15 years, since Mrs Thatcher, before she became leader, determined to abolish the rates. But it really ignited when legislation to introduce the community charge – or poll tax, as it irresistibly came to be called – went through the Commons. A major backbench revolt sought to assert the principle of ability to pay. Then, as the bills for the new tax began to pour out of council offices, MPs' postbags swelled with more complaints than many of them had ever seen before. There was no lack of rebellious Tories to say, 'I told you so.'

This dispute had that rare incendiary quality which simultaneously lights up both parliament and the population at large. Ministers had said that the average poll tax bill in England should be for £278. The actual average turned out to be £363. Many with an obligation to pay failed to register. Others simply withheld payment. Large demonstrations took place in various parts of the country, and in some at least the political left was joined by Conservative voters. One London demonstration in March led to widespread damage to property, and 340 arrests.

Months after the worst of the storm had passed, a minister confessed that Conservative MPs had gone through a collective nervous breakdown at the time when opinion polls and their postbags told the same story of impending doom. Because the prime minister was so personally identified with reform of local government finance, many Tory MPs blamed her. Some argued that if the party was to avoid an electoral debacle, Michael Heseltine should replace her.

For a time his position seemed strong, for two reasons. The obvious one was that he was outside the government, and therefore untainted by the decision to introduce a poll tax. But more specifically, as secretary of state for the environment in Mrs Thatcher's early years, he had ruled out this method of raising local revenue. So he was free to argue in debates that it was unfair, and all but unworkable. Heseltine was careful to avoid any direct challenge to the prime minister, but no Conservative can have doubted that he was available if the call came.

Tory anxieties were aggravated in March, when Labour had its best by-election victory since 1935. In Mid-Staffordshire, a Conservative majority of 14,654 was turned into a Labour one of 9,449, a swing of 21 per cent. Although inflation, mortgages and deficiencies in the health service played some part in the campaign, the message from the doorsteps was clear: the poll tax was potentially the most disastrous vote-loser in the history of this government.

Local government elections were due in May and, among many Conservative councillors, feelings were close to panic. That mood quickly transmitted itself, through the party organisation and through already worried MPs, to the government. The prime minister promised that there would be a review of the working of the poll tax, and established a cabinet committee under her own chairmanship to look for a vote-saving compromise.

The local elections produced about 300 Labour gains, on top of gains in the same seats the previous time they had been fought. Such a defeat on top of a previous defeat is usually taken as an ominous sign for a governing party, and indeed Conservative losses of nearly 200 seats were not negligible. But they held on to two heavily reported London councils, Westminster and Wandsworth. A combination of brilliant public relations by the party chairman, Kenneth Baker, and the proximity of both boroughs to the headquarters of the news media gave them unusual prominence. Tory MPs were ready to be calmed down, and Baker and the party whips succeeded in calming them.

Not that this change in mood solved the political problem of the poll tax. It merely brought breathing space. Chris Patten, widely regarded as one of the wisest Tory heads, had achieved what many thought belated promotion to the cabinet as environment secretary. His important long-term task was to provide the Conservatives with a policy on 'green issues', and this was a challenge he relished, for national as well as party reasons.

But it was no secret that Patten had been one of the cabinet majority who were deeply sceptical about the poll tax. He saw his immediate task as being to take the electoral sting out of the issue by consigning it to the back burner. But the prime minister did not want to give councils large sums of taxpayers' money, which she feared they would not use to reduce voters' bills. For a time, she favoured new legislation to give the government wider capping powers.

Chris Patten, whose decision to cap twenty councils this year was supported by the courts, just at the time the cabinet committee was conducting its review, argued that he already had wide enough powers. He feared another poll tax bill would provoke controversy right through the winter and spring, with endless revolts and alarms at Westminster. In the end, he persuaded the prime minister to avoid primary legislation, and was given a priority allocation of extra funds in the autumn public spending negotiations, in the hope that this would maintain next year's poll-tax bills at reasonable levels. He said it should. Many council organisations said that was impossible.

Towards the end of the year, ministers began to hope they had reduced the electoral damage, or would have done so if the economy came right well before the election – a rather big 'if'. For, with inflation in double figures again, and after all the pain of the Thatcher years, Ministers found themselves back with the same inflationary trend they had inherited in 1979.

Most of them believed that, as people became used to the new local government tax, and as Whitehall blamed future increases on councils, the really dangerous political issue was not poll tax, but mortgages. One cabinet member reported an incident at a constituency surgery where a woman was worried about an *annual* increase of £150 from rates to poll tax. But she had also suffered an increase of £150 a *month* in her mortgage.

The minister hoped that if John Major could get interest rates, and therefore mortgages, down before the election, the poll tax would be, if not forgotten, then largely forgiven.

While Labour exploited Conservative troubles, its own deliberations on an alternative showed how difficult it is to reform local government finance. The first proposal of its environment team, led by Bryan Gould, leaked out. It was for a property-based tax, like the rates, together with an element based on income. The Conservatives, smarting from their own difficulties,

Neil Kinnock spells out the new Labour message at a rally in London.

called this 'two taxes for one'. Later, impressed by the monosyllabic effectiveness of attacks on their own 'poll tax', they labelled Labour's proposal a 'roof tax'.

Battle was joined, and the opposition eventually judged it prudent to let the government reveal the results of its review before unveiling its considered alternative. This was disclosed in a background paper, *Fair Rates*, which was vigorously debated at a special shadow Cabinet meeting. It proposed a return to rates in the first full financial year of a Labour government, with an extension of rebates, and a rolling programme of revaluation.

Bryan Gould's environment team managed to keep in the Labour programme a longer-term commitment to see if the means-tested rebates could be replaced by an automatic calculation of liability. In other words, a use of the Inland Revenue's computerisation of income-tax records to inject 'ability to pay' into Labour's property-based tax. The Liberal Democrats, meanwhile, had gone the whole hog, and come out for a local income tax.

Labour's policy-making generally veered towards the cautious, rather than the daring. Most party leaders preferred to ride their lead in the opinion polls, and particularly the worst wave of hostility Margaret Thatcher had ever suffered. In 1989, many had been unwilling to take too much notice of the movement in polls. One said that he would not begin to feel confident of election victory until Labour had held a double-digit lead for a year. By the end of 1990, with a few blips, that had more or less happened. What was most encouraging for Labour was that many in the C2 socio-economic group (skilled manual workers), whose desertion to Mrs Thatcher in 1979 had given her victory, and sustained her ever since, appeared to have moved back to Labour in large numbers.

Some Labour insiders were less excited by the size of their lead – which had gone as high as 23 per cent in BBC *Newsnight*'s poll of polls for April – than with the consistency of their own party's support. In the last few months of 1989 and through most of 1990, Labour's poll figure moved into the upper forties, and stayed there. For three months in the spring, it even went into the fifties, though this was acknowledged to be a flash in the pan, reflecting the worst of the government's troubles over the poll tax. Few doubted that the election of 1991 or 1992 would be much more evenly contested than that of 1987.

The Liberal Democrats struggled hard throughout the year to shrug off the damage done by their period of

'The idea that Gerald Kaufman and myself turned up at the Pentagon in order to sit a kind of eleven-plus on defence policy would be ridiculous. That is not how the Americans regard it and it is not how we regard it.'
Neil Kinnock on his visit to Washington

David Owen, whose SDP ceased trading as a national party after the May local elections.

quarrelling after the 1987 election, and the subsequent merging of Liberal and Social Democratic parties. Although David Owen's decision that his SDP could not sustain itself nationally was welcome, Paddy Ashdown's efforts to win back lost ground faced frequent frustration. The Green challenge, so strong in 1989, had faded, but this remained an alternative for potential Liberal Democrat voters.

With the SLD poll rating consistently in high single or low double figures, the third party's task in the next election looked formidable. As Ashdown struggled to define a new identity which voters could recognise and

'You have to realise, sadly, that our membership is not large enough to lay claim to be a democratic party.'

Dr David Owen on the end of the SDP

support, most psephological discussion centred on where defecting supporters of the old Alliance had found a new political home (however temporary or permanent). Many used a rule of thumb, that they had gone two to one to Labour. Some Conservatives hoped, semi-secretly, that the SLD might win them back in the same proportion.

Another problem for the Liberal Democrats was that the two major parties had rediscovered the importance of the middle ground. After a long period in which Thatcherism had prospered on a right-wing programme, and Labour had failed to prosper with one dominated by the left, both decided that their battle was becoming close enough to justify compromises that might just pick up uncommitted votes.

Neil Kinnock had fought his major battles: to drop unilateral nuclear disarmament; to assert independence of the trade unions; to try to make Labour appear more European than the Tories; and to embrace market economics.

Throughout 1990, Labour leaders debated privately how much they should concentrate on attacking the government; how much on spelling out their own policies. Neil Kinnock and John Smith were against too much detail, believing this would give Conservatives

Paddy Ashdown in pensive mood looking for an elusive Liberal Democrat breakthrough.

more scope for counter-attack, and for diverting attention from the government's own troubles. But Roy Hattersley and Bryan Gould favoured more positive projection of Labour's policies, fearing that if Tory fortunes turned up before polling day, Labour's vote might not be firm enough.

This was a difference in emphasis, rather than in direction. It is a long time since a Labour leadership has been so united. But then, it is a long time since Labour has remained so high in the polls for so long. Critics argued that this was an artificial success, that when Labour's policies came under closer scrutiny before the election, the bubble would burst.

The Conservatives had been further unsettled by the involuntary loss of three more cabinet ministers. The year had scarcely begun when Norman Fowler told the prime minister he wanted to devote more time to his young family. A couple of months later, Peter Walker, one of the last survivors of Mrs Thatcher's first cabinet, gave a similar reason for his retirement.

Nicholas Ridley's departure in July was more turbulent. An unkind critic said that, while he 'had nothing against Nick's family', he hoped the trade secretary would spend more time with them. Ridley had been disappointed when he was not given the treas-

Nicholas Ridley, former trade and industry secretary, who reluctantly resigned from Mrs Thatcher's government.

ury on Nigel Lawson's departure. As the last senior Thatcherite in the cabinet, he was deeply unhappy about developments in Europe. When, in an interview in *The Spectator*, he compared the power of the European Commission with that of Hitler, the furore was so great that the prime minister reluctantly let him go.

An anomaly of the Thatcher years, which became more pronounced in 1990, is that the most right-wing Conservative prime minister since Neville Chamberlain has not succeeded in producing a credible right-wing candidate to compete for the succession when she goes. By the end of 1990, none of the most probable successors was a true Thatcherite. They were: Douglas

Hurd (if death or ill-health removed the prime minister before the election); Michael Heseltine (still in with a chance if she is defeated by Labour); and John Major, Chris Patten and Kenneth Baker, depending on how their reputations stand if the Tories win, and Mrs Thatcher retires after a couple of years.

Yet by the end of 1990, any thought of an early change in the Conservative leadership had receded, and Michael Heseltine was left to wait upon events. With the economy and the polls both looking grim, but with the worst of the poll-tax storm apparently over, the party had settled for the long haul. Tory nerves were much more steady, though MPs also waited upon events.

'I would like to spend more time with my large but still young family.'
Peter Walker resigning as secretary of state for Wales

'After over ten years as a minister . . . I should be able to devote more time to my own family.'
Norman Fowler resigning as secretary of state for employment

'The last thing I want to do is spend more time with my family.'
Nicholas Ridley, resigning as secretary of state for trade and industry

VOTING
for POWER

By-election swings and public polls

put Labour into the lead, but

the people supported the government

for its stand against Iraq's invasion

of Kuwait

Peter Snow

N ineteen ninety was undoubtedly Labour's year but, as it drew to a close, it was by no means certain the party was set to win the approaching general election.

It was the year which presented Labour with its biggest opportunity since Mrs Thatcher came to power. The economic slowdown was hurting everyone: if you had a mortgage you were crippled by high interest rates and you only had to visit a supermarket once a month to notice the inexorable climb in prices. It wasn't the hyper-inflation of the early Eighties but everyone felt it, and most blamed the government. And for the first time in a decade voters could look across at the opposition benches in the House of Commons and see a Labour party that looked competent, united and electable. The Greens were fading, the Liberal Democrats, though fighting doughtily, were still failing to win back the ground the Alliance had abandoned. For the first time in a decade, Labour had unrivalled command of the opposing trenches on the battleground. Yet somehow Mrs Thatcher's Conservative government did not have that sense of decay about it that signals the end of a political era. It would be a brave person – casting an eye over the arithmetic of the polls and elections of 1990 – who would bet more than a modest sum on the result of the next general election, which may still be a year and a half away.

Take the opinion polls first. These are not the real verdicts of people voting in local and parliamentary by-elections: we'll examine those later. But the polls provide a reliable measure of the trend in party support from month to month, and our BBC poll of polls gives this trend a consistency and a broad base. It is published on the first Friday of each month. It is an average, weighted for sample size, of the most recent polling, published or unpublished, carried out by the six main organisations provided that the final day of fieldwork in

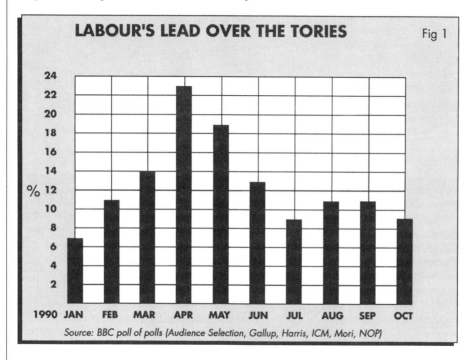

LABOUR'S LEAD OVER THE TORIES   Fig 1

Source: BBC poll of polls (Audience Selection, Gallup, Harris, ICM, Mori, NOP)

each case falls within the last fourteen days. Fig 1 shows the lead Labour had over the Conservatives for the first nine months of 1990 – when people were asked: 'If there were an election today, which party would you vote for?'

Each of Labour's monthly leads is impressive – September's particularly so in view of the massive support people were expressing for the government's handling of the early weeks of the Gulf crisis (which began with Iraq's invasion of Kuwait on 2 August – too late for August's poll of polls). Labour's 23 per cent lead in April was an all-time record gap over the Tories (tracing the BBC's poll of polls back to the last general

The BBC poll of polls is a weighted average of the latest polling – published or unpublished – done by the six main polling organisations, provided that the last day of field work falls within two weeks of the day of publication.

election in June 1987 and the monthly Gallup index before that). It coincided – as we shall see – with Mrs Thatcher's lowest rating ever in the leadership stakes, and most notably with the peak of the unpopularity of the government's poll tax. Labour managed to stay 19 per cent ahead of the Conservatives in May as well: sampling was done in the few days before the local council elections in which it was widely expected that the Conservatives would suffer a severe trouncing. But in the event the Conservatives did not do as badly as their party managers had feared and the pundits had prophesied, and Labour's lead settled down again to the commanding but hardly unstoppable 7–14 per cent it had been earlier in the year.

So what does all this tell us about prospects for the general election? Labour's target figure for an outright win is a lead of 5 per cent in the share of the vote. So the party would have been comfortably home in an election in the first nine months of 1990 if people had voted the way they responded to the pollsters. But governments historically enjoy a recovery in the lead up to elections. If the Conservatives win a typical 'swingback' of support, they should be able, at least, to deny Labour an overall majority.

This is not to ignore the crushing blow to the Conservative party's nervous system of those two massive Labour leads of April and May. It is worth recording that *no* government since polling began has ever recovered from a deficit like April's 23 per cent and gone on to win a subsequent general election. Moreover, the balance of skilled working-class voters (the C2s), who are credited by most pollsters with having been the single most decisive group to switch to the Conservatives in 1979 and stay with them, albeit in reduced numbers, through most of the Eighties, appeared by the autumn of 1990 to have returned to Labour. August's Gallup 9000 in *The Daily Telegraph* suggested that C2 support was 31 per cent for the Conservatives and 52 for Labour. Gallup's election survey had put the C2s as 31 per cent Conservative in the October 1974 election and 49 per cent Labour. This switched to 45 per cent for each party in 1979, and was still Conservative 41 per cent and Labour 33 per cent in the 1987 Gallup election survey. So if we believe Gallup, an 8 per cent Conservative lead in this key group at the time of the 1987 election had changed to a 21 per cent Labour lead by August 1990 – that's a 15 per cent swing to Labour.

The story of Labour's ascendancy in 1990 really begins with the European elections of 1989. It was the first nationwide election in which the Conservatives had been worsted since October 1974. Their share of the vote sank to 35 per cent, Labour's touched 40 per cent. Suddenly, the Labour party that Mr Kinnock had been carefully grooming for six years was a winner. The victory transformed popular perceptions of a party that had now put its house in order. In July 1989, Labour overtook the Conservatives in the BBC's poll of polls for the first time since before the 1987 general election. Through the late summer of 1989 and a carefully orchestrated party conference, in which the fruits of the party's policy review were neatly presented and dutifully voted through by mild-mannered majorities, Labour's share of public support as measured by the BBC's poll of polls rose to 48 per cent in November and 47 per cent in December. The Conservatives were rocked by a challenge to Mrs Thatcher's leadership and by the Thatcher–Lawson fight that ended in the chancellor's resignation: they were running at only 36 per cent in November and 37 per cent in December 1989. Their support would have been lower if it had not been for the failure of the Green party to maintain its momentum and the lacklustre performance of the Liberal Democrats. By the beginning of 1990, people were beginning to say that Neil Kinnock had a chance of attracting the largest net movement of votes at the approaching general election than any party had won since 1945. To win the next election his Labour party requires a swing* of over 8 per cent from the Conservative lead of 11 per cent at the 1987 general election. He was achieving swings of over 10 per cent in the polls by the end of 1989.

So when the year began – as Fig 2 shows – the BBC's poll of polls was showing Labour comfortably ahead. It was a two-horse race. Labour's job was to keep it that way, and continue to bid for the votes in the middle that had drifted to the Alliance in the last two elections, fatally dividing the opposition challenge to Mrs Thatcher. Labour party self-discipline, and the pain of rising inflation and interest rates ensured that the strategy worked. The arrival on English doorsteps of the poll-tax demands which had already infuriated much of Scotland the year before delivered the *coup de grâce.* Labour's 53 per cent in April was its best since September 1971. And its lead over the Conservatives was an all-time record. It also coincided with a parliamentary by-election gain from the Conservatives in Mid-Staffordshire which not only had the Conservative vote collapsing (that was nothing unusual) but the Labour vote soaring (and that was *very* unusual.) Labour appeared to have broken through.

'Swing' is calculated by measuring one party's lead over the other at one time, comparing it with the party lead at another time, and halving the difference. Thus in Fig 1 there was a swing to Labour of 8% between January and April 1990, and a swing to the Conservatives of 7% between April and July.

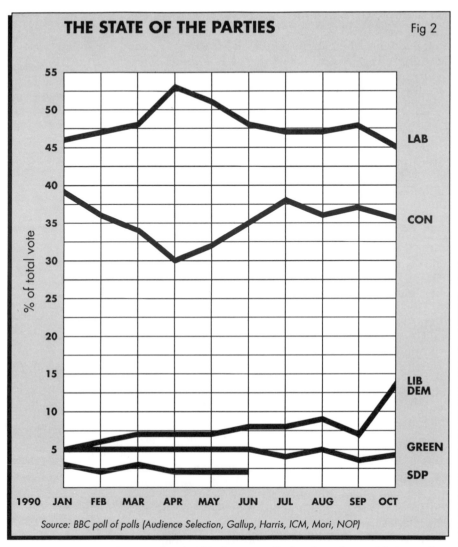

THE STATE OF THE PARTIES   Fig 2

% of total vote

LAB

CON

LIB DEM

GREEN

SDP

1990 JAN FEB MAR APR MAY JUN JUL AUG SEP OCT

Source: BBC poll of polls (Audience Selection, Gallup, Harris, ICM, Mori, NOP)

But had Labour really broken through? As spring turned to summer, Labour's lead began to ease back to a level which would have won them a general election, yet also gave the Conservatives some cheer. I well recall the night of the Bootle by-election in May (about which – together with Mid-Staffs – more later) when we were rehearsing our late night by-election special programme in the studio. On these occasions, all the excitement of the show is rightly geared to the result of the by-election where real voters are delivering their verdict – albeit in special local circumstances. But it turned out that the real news that night was not so much the predictable election of a new Labour MP for Bootle, as the fact that our poll of polls – which includes some unpublished sampling as well as the most recent published polls – saw Labour's lead drop by 6 points from the 19 per cent May figure we'd published only three weeks earlier. In that last week of May it was down to 13 per cent; it had been 23 per cent when it created new records in April, just seven weeks earlier.

By summer's end, Sir Geoffrey Howe may have overstated it when he remarked: 'Labour's brief interlude of plausibility is drawing to an end,' but Labour support, at 47 per cent in July and August and 48 per cent in September, was hardly the comfortable peak from which the party could afford to decline a few points and still be confident of victory in less favourable times to come. After all, the economic pundits seemed agreed that the second half of 1990 should be the nadir of the government's economic misfortunes. The outlook beyond that was for steadying and then falling inflation, lower interest rates and an improving balance of payments. And although at the time of going to press the Gulf crisis has induced a far greater sense of economic uncertainty, the government will have at least one, perhaps two more spring budgets in which to fine-tune the economy to its electoral advantage.

The last column in Fig 2 shows how little the first four weeks of the Gulf crisis affected the parties' positions in the poll of polls. If the Conservatives may have been hoping for something of the Falklands effect (which sent them shooting up by ten points in Gallup between April and May 1982) there was little sign of it. A Harris poll published in *The Observer* on Sunday 26 August did show the Labour lead down to 8 per cent. Only time will tell whether this poll heralded a recovery for the government at a time of acute foreign crisis. Mori's poll published in *The Sunday Times* the same day, with fieldwork a few days earlier, showed a Labour lead of 15 points, and it provided one piece of evidence for drawing an emphatic contrast with the spring of 1982: people were more gloomy about prospects for the economy than Mori could remember for ten years.

If the government was unable to draw any electoral optimism from the broad message of people's answers to the pollsters on voting intention, it had at least wholehearted backing for its stand against Iraq's occupation of Kuwait. A number of polls in August – most notably the survey carried out by NOP for the BBC *Newsnight* programme and *The Independent* newspaper and *The Sunday Telegraph*'s Gallup survey published the same day – put support for sending British troops to the Gulf at nearly 90 per cent. But there was one warning note in an answer given to NOP: 51 per cent of all those asked said they would not support the use of British and American troops to attack Iraq without UN approval.

There were four occasions before we went to press in the autumn of 1990 on which people cast real votes in real ballot boxes. The first – the Mid-Staffordshire by-election – was the most spectacular demonstration of disaffection with a Conservative government and transfer of allegiance to the Labour party that Britain had seen since 1935. Sylvia Heal, the Labour candidate, made the most of the government's economic travail and the unpopularity of the poll tax. She overturned a Conservative majority of 14,654 at the 1987 general election, forging home with 9,449 votes more than the unfortunate Tory, Charles Prior. The Liberal Democrat was left with half the votes the Alliance had won in 1987; the Social Democrat, the Green and nine other candidates all lost their deposits. Labour (Fig 3) were up 25 per cent on their general election share, the Liberal Democrats down 12 per cent and the Conservatives down 18 per cent. It was a 21 per cent swing to Labour. A swing of 8 per cent would win Labour a general election. It looked like the return of two-party politics.

MID-STAFFORDSHIRE BY-ELECTION
22 MARCH

Sylvia Heal (Lab)	27,649
Charles Prior (Con)	18,200
Timothy Jones (Lib Dem)	6,315
Ian Wood (SDP)	1,422
Robert Saunders (Official Green)	1,215
James Bazeley (Anti-Thatcher Con)	547
Lord David Sutch (Monster Raving Loony)	336
Christopher Hill (National Front)	311
Christopher Abell (NHS Supporters)	102
Others	191

Labour Majority: 9,449
Swing to Labour: 21.33%   Turnout: 77.5%

General Election 1987:
B.J. Heddle (Con) 28,644; C.R. St Hill (Lab) 13,990;
T.A. Jones (L/All) 13,114.
Conservative majority 14,654.

Then came the local elections on 3 May. All the London boroughs were up, as well as a number of English and Welsh districts and all the Scottish regions. Everyone had prophesied a government disaster. For Mrs Thatcher herself a severe electoral setback in the town halls was being signposted as the likely trigger for a party revolt far graver than the one she'd faced the previous November. Conservative morale had not been so low since the dog days of 1981 when the party's backbenches had been brisk with talk of mutiny. If the leader herself was blamed in advance for what promised to be a roasting at the polls, so was her community charge – the dreaded poll tax. It had helped drive Conservative support in Scotland to below 20 per cent in recent opinion polls – a level at which it is hard to imagine more than four or five of the present ten Scottish Tory MPs surviving a general election.

And yet, when the counts were in, the Conservatives, though badly beaten nearly everywhere, were able to heave a massive sigh of relief. They had held on to, and even improved their position, in two frontline London boroughs where they had kept the poll tax low. Although Labour had gained Bradford, another government flagship council, their overall share of the vote,

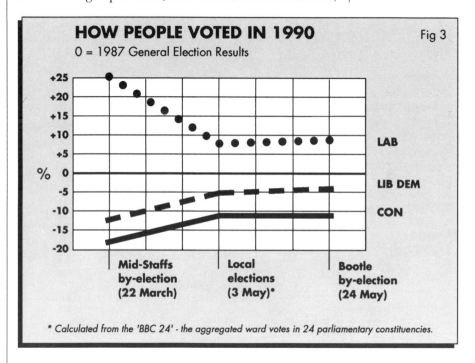

HOW PEOPLE VOTED IN 1990   Fig 3

0 = 1987 General Election Results

LAB

LIB DEM

CON

Mid-Staffs by-election (22 March)

Local elections (3 May)*

Bootle by-election (24 May)

*Calculated from the 'BBC 24' - the aggregated ward votes in 24 parliamentary constituencies.

calculated from the BBC's 24 parliamentary constituency counts, put Labour only 8 per cent up on the 1987 general election, and the Conservatives 11 per cent down. The Conservatives' local election share was precisely their level of support in the BBC's May poll of polls (see Fig 2), but Labour's 8 per cent advance in the local elections was a lot less than the 19 per cent advance in the opinion polls that put them on 51 per cent in May's poll of polls.

The other surprise was the performance of the third party. The Liberal Democrats achieved 14 per cent of the actual vote (as calculated in *The Economist* count) and 18 per cent in the BBC's estimate of its likely national vote. Since the BBC's estimate was based on votes only in seats the Liberal Democrats chose to contest, it may have slightly over-estimated their likely performance if they'd been represented everywhere. Nevertheless, by either reckoning, they did a lot better than their rating in the national opinion polls. The Liberal Democrats hailed the result as proof of their revival after two years of recrimination between the parties of the old Alliance. Others said it was just the third party making its usual above-average showing in votes at local level.

The local elections allow us one further measure of the way party loyalties have changed since the last general election. There were significant regional variations. Labour did best in the south of England outside London: swings of 18 per cent were registered in the parliamentary seat of Southampton Test and 17 per cent in Brighton Kemptown – two places where Labour has to come back at the next general election if it is to score an overall majority. In the Midlands also, Labour's vote was well up on 1987, but less so in the North; and it was actually down a fraction in Scotland. Londoners returned a mixed verdict, but there was some relic of the old 'London effect' that has left Labour weak in one of the two critical regions in the country where the next election will be won or lost.

The next electoral test was in Upper Bann in Northern Ireland. The death of the Ulster Unionist Harold McCusker resulted in a by-election that produced a disappointing message for British parties contemplating intervention in the electoral quagmire of Ulster. Colette Jones, standing as a Conservative, asked people to desert their usual sectarian-based electoral habits. She failed dismally with just 1,038 votes, a mere 3 per cent of the total. It was an embarrassment for the Conservatives who had campaigned vigorously on Colette Jones's behalf. It was the first time the Conservatives had stood independently of the Unionists for 70 years. They excused the rebuff on the grounds that Tory politics had had only three weeks of campaigning to establish a separate presence in Ulster.

Then, on 24 May, came Bootle. It was a safe Labour seat, and there was for Labour a danger that the low poll (only 50 per cent turned out to vote) would see their safe majority take a dive. But it slipped by less than 1,000 when nearly 17,000 fewer people actually voted. Labour took 75 per cent of the share – 9 per cent up on their showing in 1987. The Conservatives were 11 per cent down with just 3,220 votes. Labour's majority was 23,517. A safe seat had been decisively held. The most dramatic outcome of an otherwise unremarkable result and the main reason for Bootle entering the history books was what happened to Dr David Owen's SDP. The SDP's Jack Holmes scored 155 votes, just 0.4 per cent of the total. Lord Sutch's Monster Raving Loony Cavern Rock party had three times as many. It was the end of the SDP. David Owen announced the SDP's abandonment of any national pretensions to power, and the party disappeared from the charts, and our BBC poll of polls, with a final showing of 2 per cent in June.

And what of the fortunes of the party leaders in 1990? Mrs Thatcher's rating fell to its worst low ever, but the others failed to make capital out of this, and Neil Kinnock drifted down in spite of his party's buoyant popularity. The two of them took a boost from the Gulf crisis in September, but only time will tell if this represents a lasting revival.

The BBC's poll of polls shows Mr Kinnock failing to leap with his party to the record heights of April and May and falling back down to the upper thirties in the summer. The fact is that, although his party was in 1990 receiving more consistent support than at any other time since he succeeded Michael Foot in the autumn of 1983, Mr Kinnock has seen better days. He was for a period of more than a year – from October 1985 to November 1986 – above 40 per cent for all but three months and above 45 per cent for five months, when his party was down in the upper thirties. For most of 1990 the position was reversed, with Mr Kinnock trailing behind his party. In a Gallup survey for Thames Television, carried out when Labour was at the height of its popularity in April, Mr Kinnock scores highly as a 'vote winner' for the Labour party, who 'communicates well' and is warm and friendly. He is also, as other polls have demonstrated, given much credit for uniting and managing his party. However, when people are asked to give their verdict about what you might broadly called his *gravitas*, the amount of weight and authority that people believe he would bring to the management of the high affairs of state, he does not score highly. More people believed the economy would suffer than believed it would prosper under Mr Kinnock's leadership. More people believed Britain's reputation abroad would be reduced rather than enhanced by his leadership, and he scores unremarkably when people are asked if he's strong, decisive and controlled.

Mrs Thatcher has her problems too. The most obvious of them is that 23 per cent in May 1990 – the lowest ever recorded prime ministerial rating. The

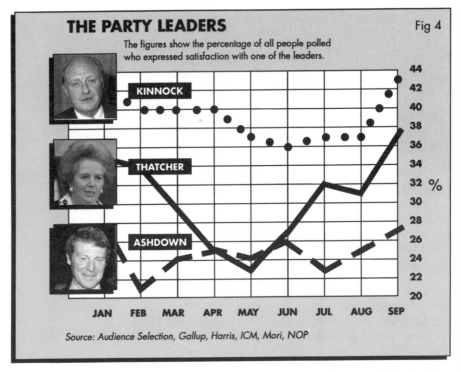

THE PARTY LEADERS   Fig 4

The figures show the percentage of all people polled who expressed satisfaction with one of the leaders.

KINNOCK

THATCHER

ASHDOWN

JAN FEB MAR APR MAY JUN JUL AUG SEP

Source: Audience Selection, Gallup, Harris, ICM, Mori, NOP

Dr David Owen, the SDP leader, began the year with a 26% rating and dropped to 22% by June, the last month his party was registered in the polls.

prime minister has always scored powerfully for her sincerity, determination and conviction. But surveys carried out in 1990 began to show that more and more people felt that the time had come for her to hand over the baton to a successor. Gallup in April and again in July gave people three choices of statement about Mrs Thatcher. Here is how they replied:

She has always been a good prime minister and she is still a good prime minister today.

April: 22 per cent   July: 27 per cent

She was once a good prime minister but she is not a good prime minister any longer.

April: 48 per cent   July: 39 per cent

She was never a good prime minister and is still not a good prime minister.

April: 26 per cent   July: 31 per cent.

This shows how deep was the disillusion with Mrs Thatcher among those who had once admired her. April's figures coincide with the period in the early spring when the poll tax was being cited as the most important issue by a very large number of people, and it was closely associated with Mrs Thatcher. Even by July, when the poll tax was no longer the dominant issue, the total of those who believed she was no longer a good prime minister totalled 70 per cent. Her moment of greatest danger, when a renewed leadership bid by one of her opponents in the party was the subject of intense backbench gossip, was in the weeks leading up to the local elections on 3 May. The relief of the party at escaping the universal electoral massacre it had expected, and the disappointing reception her chief rival Michael Heseltine won for his published alternative to the poll tax blunted the threat to her leadership. With the sudden eruption of the Gulf crisis in August, and the awareness that the country and its leader were involved in a national emergency, a challenge to her leadership became a political impossibility.

What about the issues that matter to people? The Gallup survey at the time of the 1987 general election ranked these as the most important issues: top was unemployment (49 per cent mentioned it as either their most important or second most important concern); second was defence (35 per cent); third, the NHS (32 per cent); fourth, education (19 per cent); and fifth, pensions (10 per cent). The poll tax (unsurprisingly) was not mentioned: if it was a gleam in Mrs Thatcher's eye, not many noticed it. The cost of living was mentioned by 6 per cent, and housing by a mere 5 per cent. By July 1990, people's concerns had changed dramatically. Gallup listed the issues as follows (1987 survey figures in brackets): first, the cost of living, mentioned by 35 per cent (6 per cent); second, the poll tax, 29 per cent (0 per cent); third, the NHS, 25 per cent (32 per cent); fourth, unemployment, 21 per cent (49 per cent); and fifth, housing, mentioned by 13 per cent (5 per cent). The most obvious switch is the disappearance of defence as an issue by the early autumn of 1990 (though the Gulf crisis may have aroused interest again in an issue that usually benefits the Conservatives) and its replacement by the cost of living. Although the so-called 'caring' issues like the NHS and unemployment were receding a little by the autumn of 1990, they had been overtaken by popular concern with an issue that looked far more dangerous to the government. High interest rates and inflation edging towards 10 per cent had put 'cost of living' back on top, and opinion research analysts are now convinced of the close correlation between people's gloom about the economy and their readiness to vote against the government.

Which leaves us with a final question: if most people by the autumn of 1990 were feeling negative about the government, and gloomy about prospects for the economy, were they ready to take a positive view of Labour's chances of handling things any better? Labour ranks well on most issues. On only two are the

Conservatives, in spite of their low level of national support, still the uncontested champions: defence, which fell away as an issue soon after the 1987 election; and law and order – low on people's list of priorities. But there is a third broad area – the running of the economy – where the verdict of the polls is still very mixed and uncertain, and it is in electoral terms the most important area of all.

An NOP poll for BBC's *Newsnight* and *The Independent* newspaper in July suggested that more people thought prices would go up faster under Labour than under the Conservatives. Moreover, 39 per cent of all

Author Peter Snow, BBC election guru.

those asked thought the economy would be weaker under Labour, and only 20 per cent thought it would be stronger. But Gallup's July figures give Labour a marginal 2 per cent edge over the Conservatives on the economy (when you subtract the 36 per cent who believe the Conservatives could handle it best from the 38 per cent who believe Labour could). On inflation, Labour had a lead of 6 per cent and on interest rates, 11 per cent. When people were asked: 'Taking everything into account, do you think you and your family would be better off under a Labour government than you are now, worse off, or would it not make any difference?' 38 per cent said they'd be better off, 30 per cent said they'd be worse off, 27 per cent said it would make no difference and 5 per cent didn't know. For the Labour party, which has struggled to regain public trust in its competence to run the nation's affairs, this small advantage on the issues that matter is important. But will it grow into a decisive lead as the election draws closer, or will the lower inflation and falling interest rates that are expected in 1991 give the edge back to the Conservatives?

BRITAIN'S ECONOMY

Record high interest rates and European

monetary union were the twin preoccupations

of John Major, chancellor of the exchequer,

as the spending boom of the previous

two years slowed down

Peter Jay

This has been the year of John Major. On 27 October 1989, he became chancellor of the exchequer, after a few weeks as the newly appointed foreign secretary, in an atmosphere of drama and crisis following the sudden resignation of his predecessor, Nigel Lawson, in disgust at the refusal of the prime minister to dispense with the advice of Professor Sir Alan Walters.

Mr Lawson had raised the key base rate of short-term interest to 15 per cent earlier that month in recognition of the continuing strong inflationary pressures in the economy and resulting pressure on sterling. The first important decision which Mr Major had to make almost immediately was whether to raise base rates again to 16 per cent, as suggested to him by the treasury. His decision to reject this option said much about the man and set the context for economic policy thereafter, maybe for a very long time thereafter. It is important to understand the pros and cons at that moment.

The immediate reactions of financial markets to Mr Lawson's resignation were bad. The pound fell to its lowest level against the Deutschmark since March 1987. A hike in interest rates could have been plausibly presented as justified by these short-term pressures and by the need to demonstrate that the new chancellor was at least as valiant against inflation as his illustrious predecessor. There was, moreover, a powerful political argument for seizing the opportunity to get decisively up-wind of the inflationary threat, thereby ensuring that the worst of the inevitable economic slowdown would be experienced in 1990, in time to make 1991 a year of fiscal and monetary relaxation in preparation for an election in the autumn of that year, eight or nine months before the last possible date. The immediate unpopularity of such a move could be laid at the door of the departed previous chancellor for having allowed

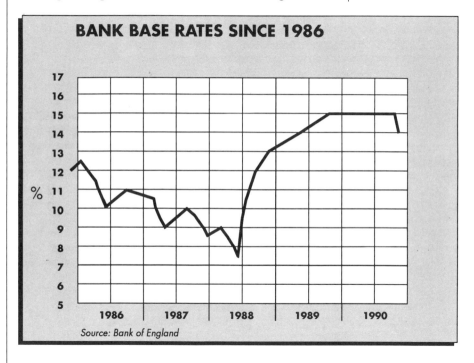

BANK BASE RATES SINCE 1986

Source: Bank of England

such an excessive spending boom to build up in 1988 and 1989; and Mr Major could have evoked the Dunkirk spirit from government backbenchers, a call to which they respond most reflexively.

Mr Major rejected the invitation. It does not seem that he was influenced by fear of the short-term unpopularity of yet another imposition on the much aggrieved mortgage interest-payer, keenly sensitive politician though he is. Rather he instinctively disliked the cynicism of blaming his predecessor, whose colleague he had been not long before as chief secretary to the treasury. More seriously, he was not convinced that higher interest rates were really necessary; and he disliked inflicting pain on the unemployed and others less well-off unless he was sure it was inevitable. This revealed two very important things about the new chancellor, which were to provide the key to understanding his actions on several subsequent occasions.

First, he had something which in an earlier and kindlier, perhaps 'wetter', age would have been called a social conscience. Secondly, he had a tendency in economic matters to look on the bright side. Commentators long in the tooth of Britain's post-war economic failings and disappointments suspected that these qualities were fatal disqualifications for a successful

Chancellor of the exchequer John Major leaves Downing Street to present his first budget.

chancellorship; but only history, still unmade, will be the judge of that.

By the turn of the year 1989–90, it seemed that the chancellor's nerve was being vindicated. The pound and financial markets rallied strongly round new year; and, more importantly, there was persuasive evidence that the economy had slowed down dramatically in the second half of 1989, that imports were running almost flat and that exports were surging ahead to the strong markets in continental Europe, even if 1989 as a whole still ended up with the largest peace-time balance of payments deficit in British history.

By the time that the chancellor had to make his

final decision about his budget, delivered on 20 March 1990, the outlook was, as so often, ambiguous. The strength of the financial markets at new year had evaporated. The trade figures for January had been dreadful and put an initial question mark over the more optimistic interpretation of the trend of imports at the end of 1989. Worst of all, the evidence about inflation gave little short-term confidence that the undoubted slowdown of the economy in the second half of 1989 was yet having any visible effect on the onward march of retail prices or on a going rate for pay settlements edging closer and closer to 10 per cent. The consensus of conventional economic opinion, no doubt with its usual experience-led bias to gloom, was that the chancellor needed to raise taxes by about £2 billion in the budget to be on the safe side.

There were, however, complications for the treasury, as well as for outsiders, about the logic of this hunch. To explain this a word must be said about 'monetarism' and its legacy. Properly understood 'monetarism' means one thing and one thing only, namely that the course of inflation is uniquely determined, after a time lag of a year or two, by changes in the amount of money in circulation. A 'monetarist' policy means – and only means – controlling changes in the amount of money in circulation with the sole purpose of accomplishing after the normal lag a target rate of inflation, eg, nil or decreasing from an initially high level to a lower or more 'acceptable' level.

There is not and never has been anything in monetarist theory in this sense that says that a monetarist policy, even if successful, will have any other desired effects than the target rate of inflation or that it will solve any other economic problems, 'real' or monetary, which cause concern, such as high unemployment, slow growth or regional imbalance. It is a simple and narrow piece of economic mechanics with absolutely no ideological or 'political' content, which if correct is equally true as a matter of fact for the practitioners of all possible political ideologies, whether Marxist or capitalist, centrally planned or free market, interventionist or laissez-faire.

Monetarist policies in Britain began with Denis Healey's speech in Leeds in January 1975, when he announced that the authorities would progressively reduce year by year the annual growth in the money supply – his predecessor Lord Barber having doubled the money supply in three and a half years – towards non-inflationary levels and that, henceforth, it would be up to trade unions to decide whether or not, against

Shadow chancellor, John Smith, leads Labour's attack on the government's handling of the economy.

'**Despite all the talk about bearing down on inflation, the government keeps scoring own goals. The government is to blame for increased prices for public transport, electricity, water, prescription charges and for a huge rise in council rents which is yet to come ... Now there is a new twist, a new boost to inflation, in the poll tax.'**
John Smith, Labour shadow chancellor

that background, they wished to price themselves out of their own and each other's jobs. By the spring of 1979 inflation had fallen from over 30 per cent to single figures, though it was showing signs of reaccelerating in the wake of the 'winter of discontent' breaches in pay restraint; and unemployment had risen above a million.

Monetarist policies in Britain ended with Nigel Lawson's Mansion House speech of October 1985, in which he announced the abandonment of money supply targets geared to inflation objectives and said that henceforth he would use his discretion to judge what level of interest rates was appropriate. Five years later inflation looked like being back – just – into double figures; and unemployment had fallen from over three million to well under two million.

But a legacy remained, namely the idea that fiscal policy – government taxes and spending and the balance between them – should not be used for the short-term steering of the economy, which was the proper province of interest rates, but instead should be geared to medium-term (ie, beyond the range of the normal four-year economic cycle) strategic objectives, such as a balanced budget or the repayment of government debt (known as the 'national debt'). Mr Lawson had devised and updated annually a medium-term financial strategy which embodied this idea and which had at the time of his 1989 budget prescribed a target budget surplus for 1990–91 of £10 billion.

By the time Mr Major came to do his final budget sums in the first quarter of 1990, it was evident that the actual surplus in 1990–91, if taxes were not changed, was likely to be £7.3 billion. General government expenditure was expected to be about £7.5 billion higher in 1990–91 than Mr Lawson had planned for that year at the time of his 1989 budget, mainly because of the extra elbow-room the cabinet had given spending ministers in the public expenditure survey exercise announced the previous autumn. Receipts were expected to be up by abut £3.6 billion; and technical adjustments contributed another £1 billion or so.

The medium-term financial strategy therefore appeared to require that taxes be increased in the budget by about £2½ billion in order to restore the previously planned £10 billion surplus for 1990–91. There was also considerable independent opinion at the time from those who were not entirely willing to abandon the use of fiscal policy as part of the mix of short-term policy instruments that a fiscal tightening of £2 billion to £3 billion was required in order to get firmly upwind of inflation, especially given the chancellor's unwillingness to raise interest rates.

At this point a certain elasticity seems to have entered into the government's interpretation of its medium-term financial strategy. 'Not using fiscal policy for short-term steering of the economy' could either mean adhering to the previously planned budget surplus, which was itself supposedly related to the strategic goal of reducing the national debt, or it could be interpreted as requiring the chancellor not to make any changes in tax rates, whatever the prospective budget surplus, at least provided that the surplus did not actually turn into a deficit.

This, of course, left a very high degree of discretion in the chancellor's hands, not dissimilar from that which had been traditionally exercised by chancellors who were quite avowedly trying to steer the short-term movements of the economy in the pre-monetarist era before 1975. Mr Major exercised this discretion fully and decided on a more or less neutral budget, raising receipts in 1990–91 by just £430 million compared with the indexed base, ie, with what receipts would have been if he had just applied the adjustments to income tax allowances and excise duties required to neutralise the effects of inflation over the previous twelve months on the real tax burden.

Once again, Mr Major had rejected the opportunity to take out an insurance policy against inflation persisting more strongly than he hoped and against all the other hazards of economic policy, such as unexpectedly bad trade figures, which can blow an optimistic economic policy off course and force the authorities to take crisis measures in order to defend the pound. Cautious observers with long memories admired his courage, but doubted his wisdom. Once again the decisive factor seems to have been Mr Major's personal reluctance to inflict more economic pain than he could be certain was needed.

In April, May and June evidence steadily mounted that the economy was not slowing down as much as the chancellor had expected in the budget or as much as was needed to maintain the necessary downward pressure on inflation. Indeed, it appeared that, after a marked slow-down in the second half of 1989, home spending and output were reaccelerating in the first half of 1990. Gross domestic product figures for the first quarter of 1990 showed an annual rate of real increase of 3 per cent over the previous quarter; and the buoyancy of imports, of retail sales and of consumer borrowing, all hinted that something might need to be done if inflation was to be brought down decisively.

After the budget and the spring decisions of local authorities about poll-tax levels, on top of the strong continuing trend of pay settlements close to 10 per cent, it was known that the so-called headline rate of inflation, as measured by the change over twelve months in the general retail price index, would rise from the 7 per cent rate early in the year to about 10 per cent by the summer. But the chancellor's hope in the budget was that this number would begin to fall in the autumn, getting back down to about 7 per cent by the end of the year and falling more rapidly in 1991, encouraged by the cuts in interest rates, and therefore in mortgage interest, which he hoped he would be able to make by that time.

As sundry political decisions – the indexing of excise duties in the budget, increases in regulated public utility prices, the poll tax and delayed effects of the increase to 15 per cent in interest rates in October 1989 – were known to have pushed up the headline inflation figure, commentators and the chancellor himself began to focus attention on what was called the underlying rate of inflation, which, it was argued, gave a fairer picture of what was really happening to inflation as a marketplace phenomenon. There were various ways of measuring this, including the chancellor's preferred method – the retail price index excluding the effects of poll tax and mortgage interest – and the gross domestic product deflator.

However it was measured, it was apparent by mid-summer that underlying inflation was also rising, though at a level about 3 per cent lower than the headline rate. For example, in the twelve months to June 1990, the headline rate was 9.8 per cent, while the underlying rate, as defined by the chancellor, was 6.9 per cent. The underlying rate was also expected to peak lower than and at about the same time as the headline rate, ie, at about 8 per cent rather than just over 10 per cent.

But there was a catch. Just because the underlying rate excluded the effects of mortgage interest and the poll tax, there was and is no prospect of the underlying rate benefiting from the automatic downward effects on the headline rate of the progressive expiry after twelve months of the effects of the 1989 interest rate rises and the early 1990 tax and utility price rises. Precisely because the underlying rate is a truer measure of the trend of inflation, it will only fall if the slowing down of the economy really does put effective downward pressure on pay and on prices.

Accordingly the question uppermost in economists' minds between spring and summer, though not apparently the minds of the financial markets or of the popular media, was whether a further increase in interest rates to 16 per cent would be necessary in order to get on top of inflation. The chancellor declared that he would not hesitate to raise interest rates, if it were necessary; and some outside observers thought it was. But it was also evident that political objections, especially among the government's supporters in the House of Commons, to a further rise in interest rates were very strong indeed, it being believed that, together with the first impact of the poll tax, higher mortgage interest payments were a key factor in the government's poor showing in opinion polls at that time.

This was the context in which, in about June, the idea began to surface that early entry by the pound into the common market's exchange-rate mechanism (ERM) might be an attractive option, or at least preferable to higher interest rates as a way of bearing down on the obstinately strong trend of inflation. Previously this question had been mainly discussed as an aspect of foreign – or at least European – policy.

The Bank of England's chief cashier shows off the new, smaller, five pound note.

In his resignation speech in the House of Commons on 31 October 1989, Mr Lawson had affirmed strongly that the exchange rate had a key role to play in the necessary framework of financial discipline and that the pound should enter the ERM as soon as possible. This followed, but also went further than, the compromise agreement reached between him, the prime minister and the then foreign secretary, Sir Geoffrey Howe, at the common market summit meeting in Madrid in June 1989, that the pound should enter the ERM when a number of conditions had been fulfilled, of which the most critical was that the gap between Britain's inflation rate and that of the rest of the common market should have been closed, or at least very substantially narrowed.

The prime minister and the new chancellor reiterated this Madrid position like gramophone records every time the subject was raised between November 1989, and the summer of 1990. But the idea of joining before the conditions were met, particularly the inflation condition, was gaining ground behind the scenes, especially in the treasury.

On a reasonably rigorous reading there was no prospect at all of the main, ie, inflation, Madrid condition being met in time for British entry into the ERM in the autumn of 1990 or, indeed, probably before 1992 at the earliest. It was hard to see why the prime minister should wish to stretch so signal a point of government policy to accommodate either the treasury's desire to use early ERM entry at a high rate to knock inflation on the head or the foreign office's wish to enhance Britain's influence in Europe by being influenced itself to fall in with the plans of the rest of the common market as embodied in at least stage one of Jacques Delors' three-stage scheme for eventual economic and monetary union. In case she was tempted, her former economic adviser and continuing family friend Sir Alan Walters was at hand to break his long silence on current economic policy in July 1990, and to draw attention to what he saw as the 'awful' consequences of entering the ERM before the Madrid conditions had been met.

The City, however, convinced itself – by its well-tried technique of endless repetition – that the chancellor himself was responsible for talking the pound up by circulating rumours of an early autumn entry into the ERM and golden horizons thereafter. There was no public evidence for this, least of all in the interview he gave on 15 May to the *Wall Street Journal* that sparked off the market's first bout of euphoria, or in the later *Financial Times* story that autumn entry was indeed being planned. Mr Major stuck metronomically to the Madrid chorus in public, adding only the glosses about the underlying rate of inflation and the concept of proximation. Nor did it seem that in private he was at all pleased by the frequent suggestion that he was in some way in league with the foreign secretary to drag the prime minister into the ERM and more generally 'towards Europe'.

In June and July he delivered two very notable speeches, which bore strong hallmarks of his own thinking. On 12 June in London he launched his plan for a hard ecu; and on 6 July in North Wales he delivered a broadside attack on the central idea of the Delors plan, especially stage three, which envisaged a community-wide political decision to adopt a single currency in place of existing national currencies, by implication quite soon (?1994) after – perhaps even coincidentally with – the establishment of the single market at the end of 1992.

In theory the hard ecu would be a twelfth common market currency (twelfth, not thirteenth, because Luxemburg does not have an independent currency) which could not depreciate against any of the eleven national currencies and which the private sector – businessmen, tourists, perhaps even trades unions (though Mr Major did not mention them) – would be free to use in preference to their national currencies as they chose.

If enough of them so chose, then according to Mr Major 'in the very long term' (?2025) and if governments also so chose, national currencies could fade away leaving the common hard ecu currency as also the only single currency.

In practice, Mr Major seemed principally attracted by this scheme for what he saw as the much-neglected stage two of economic and monetary union because it would retain national currencies – and therefore the all-important safety valve of exchange-rate realignments at least as a last resort – almost indefinitely, albeit at high financial cost to any central bank whose currency was

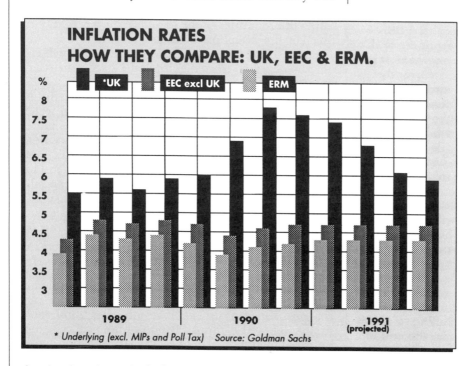

INFLATION RATES
HOW THEY COMPARE: UK, EEC & ERM.

% •UK   EEC excl UK   ERM

* Underlying (excl. MIPs and Poll Tax)   Source: Goldman Sachs

1989   1990   1991 (projected)

devalued. Others, including evidently the governor of the Bank of England, Robin Leigh-Pemberton, saw the hard ecu as genuinely a stepping stone – and a better one than Jacques Delors' European central bank system – towards a single currency within an imaginable time scale (?2000).

Mr Major's Llandudno speech revealed much more of his own thinking, indeed of his political personality. He really hates unemployment in a way which has not been politically fashionable since the first half of the 1970s (before Denis Healey's inauguration of monetarist policies in his speech in January 1975 in Leeds). He drew a strong lesson from the experience of the United States, itself a large single-currency area, namely that even with the exceptionally high labour mobility of that country and its common language, the adjustment between different regions of the American economy to changing competitiveness commonly involved considerable pain in the form of high regional unemployment and the constrained movement of populations to other regions.

He did not say in so many words that the common market could not contemplate a single currency at least until it had a common language; but he left his Welsh CBI audience in little doubt that, when he spoke of the convergence of economic performances between the different economies of the common market that must precede the adoption of a single currency, he was speaking of fundamental factors of the kind which can only be expected to change radically over a matter of decades.

This introduced a new element into the British debate about economic and monetary union, which had previously tended to be stereotyped into a rather sterile polarity between pro- and anti-Europeans, both very diffuse concepts. Mr Major, by contrast, was addressing the issue on its economic merits, not just for Britain, but for the common market as a whole; and the arguments he made were not arguments particularly about Britain or its sovereignty, but arguments which, if valid, were equally valid for all common market economies and indeed for any designer at the centre of a common market monetary system.

Indeed, since the argument was that for the common market to function successfully as a continental economy it needed the flexibility of exchange-rate changes between its main regions lest intolerable strains were to be imposed upon its political cohesion by forced migration of huge blocks of population across language and national frontiers in search of work, it was an argument that logically was more important to a pro-European, who desired the political success of the common market, than to an anti-European, who was indifferent to it and might even half-welcome such a political time-bomb planted in its economic foundations.

As parliament broke up at the end of July for its summer recess the arguments still raged both about the interpretation of the progress of the British economy and about the right European monetary order and Britain's place in it. A big fall in the official figure for retail sales in June encouraged the financial markets to believe that the 15 per cent interest rate might after all finally be having its desired effect; and the chancellor

'Inflation is the overriding problem facing the UK economy at the moment. It is currently around 7¾% and will stay above 7% for a while yet. That is too high, unacceptably high, and we must get it down. And we will get it down; the forecast published with my autumn statement foresaw retail price inflation falling to 5¾% by the end of 1990.'

John Major, chancellor of the exchequer, speaking in January

was able to cite a few other straws in the wind encouraging such hopes, such as the housing market and a small fall in producer output (or factory gate) prices in June.

The autumnal equinox brought economic gales. The Gulf crisis had more than doubled spot oil prices by late September. The triumphal mood of the July economic summit in Texas – celebrating the victory of democracy and market economics round the world – had turned to gloom and doom by the time the world's finance ministers and top bankers met in Washington for the annual meetings of the IMF and World Bank.

Mr Major took to the radio in early September to quell resurgent rumours that British entry into the ERM was imminent. Likewise, he seized every opportunity before and during the IMF meetings during the last week of September to discourage hopes of an early relaxation of monetary policy, although he also used the occasion of his set-piece speech there to redefine the Madrid conditions yet again so that the convergence of British inflation with that in the rest of the common market would only require to be prospective rather than actual as the trigger for entry.

Whether it was iron nerve, masterly inactivity or disagreement with his neighbour, the chancellor was as unwilling to relax policy in the face of the gathering recession in the autumn as he had been to tighten it in the face of rising inflation in the previous winter and spring.

History may yet celebrate him for his sturdy resistance to the overwrought roller-coaster of economic confidence. Or it may condemn him, like so many of his predecessors, for doing too little, too late. Certainly, the Gulf crisis had not helped, adding perhaps 1 per cent to Britain's underlying inflation in 1991, though also doing much the same to the rest of the common market comparator for the purposes of the Madrid conditions for entry into the ERM.

An alarming CBI survey in late September, the gloomiest for nearly a decade, reinforced other evidence that the Lawson boom had finally petered out and that the long awaited economic slowdown was developing into what was variously to be called a growth recession, a cooling-off period or, indeed, a full-blooded recession. The chancellor and his opposite number, the secretary of the US treasury, Nicholas Brady, were both heard to remark during the IMF meetings that they preferred not to use the word 'recession', a sure sign that output growth would be negligible or negative for several quarters to come.

The markets reflected these shocks. The FTSE,

'It is wholly wrong to say we are off course. Certainly, it is taking a little longer to come down than we imagined.'
John Major speaking after inflation reached 9.8% in July

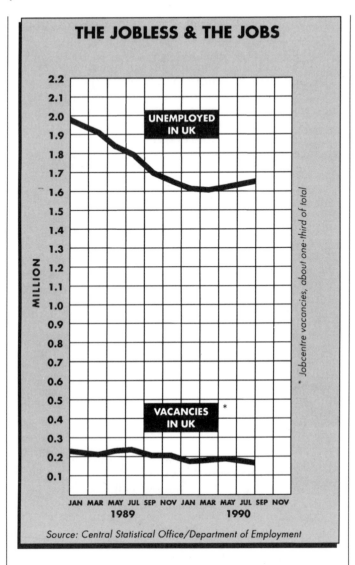

THE JOBLESS & THE JOBS

UNEMPLOYED IN UK

VACANCIES IN UK *

MILLION

* Jobcentre vacancies, about one-third of total

JAN MAR MAY JUL SEP NOV JAN MAR MAY JUL SEP NOV
1989   1990

Source: Central Statistical Office/Department of Employment

which had been pirouetting near its 2400+ peak in high summer, fell below 2000 in the last week of September. Sterling, which initially gained strongly from the Gulf crisis (the UK being an oil producer), drifted downwards in the second half of September as the market's belief in imminent ERM entry ebbed away, despite the chancellor's more upbeat hint in Washington.

But confronted with deteriorating economic conditions and the deep uncertainty of the Gulf crisis, political considerations suddenly and dramatically won the day. On 5 October, the last day of the Labour party conference, the chancellor announced that Britain would enter the ERM the following Monday, the eve of the Tory party conference.

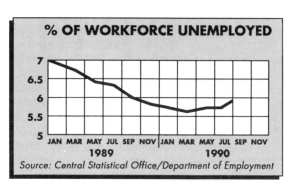

% OF WORKFORCE UNEMPLOYED

Source: Central Statistical Office/Department of Employment

A major economic issue was thus determined in a highly political manner in a primarily political context. Looking to the next election, the government was determined to get interest rates and inflation down without further deflating the economy. The immediate reaction was favourable. Share prices rose steeply. Interest rates were cut, with the promise of further cuts in the New Year. Whether ERM membership will provide John Major with the economic correction the government seeks in time for an election next year will no doubt be determined by various factors, wage inflation and the international situation in particular.

BRITAIN'S

changing

SOCIETY

The public took the ambulance workers'

side in their pay dispute and

was alarmed by the government's

proposed shake-up of the NHS,

fiercely opposed by doctors

Polly Toynbee

The National Health Service was scarcely out of the news during the year. It was the government's NHS and community care bill which caused the fiercest political battle. The bill proposed the most profound changes to the health service since the foundation of the NHS – changes that were pushed through in the teeth of ferocious opposition from virtually the whole medical establishment.

'Efficiency and caring go hand in hand,' said Kenneth Clarke on the day in November 1989 when the bill was published. Robin Cook, Labour's shadow health spokesman, replied: 'The health service in Britain is no longer going to be a public service but a business enterprise.' The public was confronted with two quite different visions of what the new plans would mean for the future of the NHS.

From April 1991, health authorities will no longer provide care, but will purchase it from hospitals for patients within their area. In a new 'internal market' system, hospitals will bid for contracts so that health authorities can shop around for the most efficient treatment. Health authorities can specify minimum quality of care and limits on waiting times in their contracts.

The idea is that badly managed, less popular, hospitals will wither away, while the best can thrive and grow. For the first time, everyone in the NHS will be forced to cost everything they do.

Because managers are years away from a true analysis of their costs, at first the contracts will be approximate – large block contracts based on rough guesstimates. The department of health has instructed health authorities in the first year to send patients to exactly the same hospitals as they were sent to last year, to avoid disruption in the early stages.

But one part of the new system, small in itself, will provide the motor that will force health authorities to be as accurate in their contracts as possible. Some hospitals can volunteer to become free-standing, self-governing NHS trusts. For them – forty or so in the first year starting in April 1991 – the contracts will be real, and the money that flows in to them from health authorities will be hard cash.

The other cornerstone of the plan where real money could flow unpredictably right from the start will be with those GPs in big practices who can now choose to hold entire budgets for their patients. They can buy hospital treatment wherever they choose for their patients, and they will be the ones who decide which of their patients gets priority in treatment from their budgets.

The plan had been drawn up by a small committee that was set in motion by Mrs Thatcher's surprise announcement of a review during a *Panorama* interview in the midst of one of the many NHS winter financial crises of 1988. Whichever government was in power, there would have been a strong incentive to try to reform the running of the NHS in some way. Half-way through each financial year the NHS hits the headlines with sudden ward and operating theatre closures as managers find their budgets overstretched. More money pours in every year, yet waiting lists rise. More doctors and nurses are hired, more operations performed, more patients treated, and still the delays grow and costs rise at well above inflation rates.

The review took place in the context of the growing doubts of some health experts about whether the state can put enough new money into the NHS indefinitely without a tax burden which will be publicly unacceptable. The public says they are willing to pay more for the NHS, but if governments offering low taxation rates continue to be the ones rewarded at the ballot box, these good intentions may never find political expression. Fears such as these made it more important than ever that the NHS should get the best value possible for every penny spent, according to the government.

The review argued that although overall the NHS looked efficient compared with some other countries, in many areas it was badly managed. No one knew what anything cost, or how large sums were spent. Consultants in hospitals often made financial decisions that had more to do with their own empire building than rational delivery of health care. Some hospitals had huge waiting lists, others nearby almost none, yet patients were referred by GPs who had no access to that information. Preliminary studies showed that treatment in one hospital could cost many times the same treatment in another.

But, the government believed, the most serious fault in the system was that the best hospitals were actually penalised for high productivity and efficiency, while the worst benefited. Hospitals doing the most operations, most quickly, with the greatest demands for their services, were the ones likely to run into the red half-way through the financial year, even if their per capita costs were low. Less good hospitals which conducted fewer operations, kept people blocked in beds unnecessarily or inappropriately, providing less all round, at higher per capita costs, could balance their books by sluggish activity. The government said that the incentives all worked in the wrong direction. And, at the same time, parts of the NHS had become unacceptably shabby and run-down, with buildings decaying and facilities sub-standard. What was gratefully accepted by patients in 1948 was not always acceptable now. As standards of living rose so did patients' expectations of what they received from the NHS.

Introducing competition within the NHS was a wholly new concept. The government said it was the only way to sharpen up the management, and encourage the best. The opposition and the doctors said that any idea of a 'market' was contrary to all the most fundamental principles of the NHS. (Indeed, after the white paper, the language of the 'market', and 'competition' was notably dropped from ministerial speeches – though the shape of the plan was hardly altered at all in response to criticisms.

Critics of the bill said that the cheapest will inevitably drive out the best in a competitive system. Patients will be sent miles away from home to hospitals where health authorities have contracted the most efficient but not necessarily the most convenient beds for patients. While Kenneth Clarke said that money would follow the patients, Robin Cook replied that the patients would be likely to find themselves following where the money has already been contracted. Clarke says there will be more patient choice; Cook and the doctors claim it will mean less.

Labour never opposed the idea of a proper costing system within the NHS. Six pilot schemes – called resource management initiatives – were already in progress, and could have been spread across the country. Labour agreed that GPs should have more information on costs and waiting lists before referring patients – but it was opposed on principle to the idea of the buying and selling of treatment within the service.

Those most afraid of the effects of the new system were the big regional hospitals and teaching centres. Take University College Hospital, London, for instance. Ninety per cent of its patients come from outside its area and it received patients last year from every single health authority in Britain. The hospital will now have to bill each health authority for each patient. But health authorities don't know how many patients are sent to hospitals such as these. They have been told to keep a reserve in their back pockets to pay for such referrals, but they don't know how much to set aside. Half-way through the year, they may find they have no money left for these referrals. University College could find suddenly that it is sent no more patients and the money dries up. The department of health has tried to reassure these hospitals that referral patterns will stay the same, at least in the first year – but that hasn't calmed the fears of many who feel health authorities will be obliged to cut their costs.

Kenneth Clarke has been reassuring nervous colleagues that he can keep the whole system running smoothly through the transition, in the dangerous period leading up to the next election. But the opposition points to the large number of possible pitfalls and financial disasters that may hit the scheme, especially now that there is far less money in the system to oil the wheels, as unexpectedly high inflation has eaten away at the extra money that would have been there. This year again, hospitals have had to make sudden cut-backs and closures in many areas where budgets were wrecked by the high rate of inflation.

By the time the bill reached the House of Commons, Conservative back-benchers, who had been deeply anxious about the whole scheme, had largely fallen into line behind Kenneth Clarke, partly because of the ferocity of the campaign waged by the British Medical Association. Tory MPs closed ranks in the face of a poster and press campaign that became a brilliantly destructive piece of political hatchet-work.

The doctors had played on the worst fears of the safety of the NHS in the hands of a Conservative government. They rarely discussed the details of the scheme but relied on the public's implicit faith in doctors and mistrust of politicians. Posters appeared up and down the country showing a frail old lady in bed; they read: 'It's not a local anaesthetic if the hospital's fifty miles away.' Dr John Marks, a North London GP, chairman of the BMA's general council, was a powerful and dogged advocate of its cause. He didn't look like a grandee consultant protecting a professional interest group but liked to present himself as a kind of cheeky chappie, a man of the people.

The BMA campaign caused a heavy loss to the government in the opinion polls, as the NHS rose to the top of the list of public concerns. The doctors won the public argument, but as many of them came to realise later, it was a hollow victory. They succeeded in damaging the government but they were not a particularly politically motivated group and they couldn't turn that damage to their advantage. The savagery of their campaign began to rebound on them when they attacked Mrs Thatcher and Kenneth Clarke personally in posters – 'What do you call a man who doesn't take medical advice? Kenneth Clarke.' But he was unlikely to take doctors' advice given via megaphone and poster. The doctors lost whatever influence they might have had with ministers in trying to alter or amend the scheme. They drove the faint hearts on the Tory backbenches safely back into the government lobby by the time the bill came to the vote in the Commons. As a result, scarcely any of the plans outlined in the white paper were significantly altered before or during the course of the bill's passage through parliament.

However, there remained wise old heads on the Conservative backbenches who kept asking themselves why the government had embarked on such a dangerous policy, in which the public would see so little benefit – or at least not for many years, during which time the Labour party would be the only winner. 'If it ain't broke, why fix it?' asked one. No government had ever come out ahead in a fight with the doctors. For the Conservative government, with its privatising reputation, it was an exceptionally dangerous issue to touch. However often ministers said the scheme had nothing to do with preparing the way for future privatisation, it was easy for the opposition to plant that fear firmly in the public mind. The NHS is a beloved and revered

Army ambulances are called in as the ambulance workers' dispute drags on.

institution, regarded as the corner-stone of what's popularly believed to be our benign cradle-to-grave welfare state system.

Public affection for the NHS flows over into a strong sympathy with most of the people who work within it. In the middle of Kenneth Clarke's struggle to persuade the public that he was on the side of the NHS and not in the business of privatising it, his troubles were multiplied by a particularly politically sensitive dispute. The ambulance workers were a group for whom there is exceptional, almost superstitious, public affection. For five long months the ambulance crews were largely off the streets in most parts of the country. Night after night Kenneth Clarke appeared on television, trying to explain why he wouldn't give a relatively small increase to a small group of very popular NHS workers.

They were not on strike – never would be, said Roger Poole, the brilliant negotiator for the combined health service unions. But lock-out or strike, the effect was the same and Roger Poole was able to claim a moral superiority for his members. His crews were not putting the public at risk, he kept saying. They were willing to work, turning up for every shift, waiting for calls that were being re-routed to the police and then to the army – a strange and sinister sight on city streets.

In September 1989, the ambulance workers had rejected a 6.5 per cent pay offer, below inflation. They wanted not only a larger increase but a pay formula that would link them to the same increases as firefighters and the police. In Roger Poole, Kenneth Clarke had found himself another formidable opponent, the most credible leader of a trades union dispute in years. His soulful eyes and his eloquence pleaded the decency of the men and women of the ambulance service. His elegant suits and ties spoke of a man a decade away from the spectacle of Arthur Scargill on the Orgreave picket lines.

Public money poured into the buckets of the ambulance crews. Opinion polls echoed that support. There could hardly be a group of workers who seemed less dangerously politically motivated. Night after night they appeared on television – disciplined orderly folk, the sort who might have joined the army or the police, but gentler.

But the government saw a serious threat. Roger Poole was also negotiator for the vast battalions of NHS workers in Nupe, Cohse and other smaller unions. The NHS is the biggest employer in Europe. Giving all its workers an extra percentage point in pay would divert considerable sums from Kenneth Clarke's scarce

'The fact that the public were supporting them and liked ambulancemen did not relieve the people responsible for the health service of making sure we spent the taxpayers' money sensibly . . . That is my overriding responsibility and I like people to judge me by the extent to which I discharge that.'
Kenneth Clarke, secretary of state for health

resources for his NHS plans. He suspected the ambulance men to be the vanguard of the whole NHS, waiting for the chance to signal a leap ahead in pay for the whole, huge, underpaid workforce.

Strong public support was the only weapon the ambulance crews had and they never lost that. But they could not convert it into a real weapon against the government. There was little sign that patients were suffering. Overall death rates in accident and emergency units did not rise during the dispute. It became clear that the government was willing to press on indefinitely, spending, some estimates suggest, £23 million on alternative services.

By February, after a hard Christmas without pay, many workers were drifting off into other jobs. New negotiations began, and both sides came out claiming victory. Instead of the original 6.5 per cent over one year, they were given 13.3 over two years. Roger Poole said he had 'driven a coach and horses through the government's public-sector pay policy'. But it was enough of a defeat to warn off other health service workers, who soon afterwards voted to accept their pay offer.

Although he won the dispute, the long drawn-out battle made it harder for Kenneth Clarke to present himself and his NHS plans in a sympathetic light. Night after night on television he was drawn into a gladiatorial fight, abrasively talking down the ambulance workers, despite public support for them.

But he did have one policy that was almost universally welcomed. Tacked somewhat uncomfortably on to the back of the NHS bill were the new community care proposals, long awaited and much praised from all sides of the House of Commons.

In 1988, Sir Roy Griffiths had published a government-commissioned report about the plight of the 6 million old, frail and handicapped people surviving at home, cared for by relatives, often with little or no help from the state. He also examined the reasons for the ten-fold increase in the cost to the state of sending people into private residential and nursing homes. His report found that most people wanted to stay at home as long as possible, and could be helped to do so, possibly more cheaply, if better local social services were provided to help them.

The Griffiths report was a powerful indictment of a system which was neither economic nor humane. Currently, responsibility falls between the social security budget centrally, local social services and the health authorities. Each tries to push people off its budget on to one of the others, with no coherent overall strategy.

'The improvement on pay is simply staggering. We have driven a coach and horses through the government's pay policy.'
Nupe negotiator Roger Poole

Roger Poole, union negotiator, heralds victory as the ambulance workers' dispute is settled.

Griffiths recommended that all money for these people should be taken from central government funds and placed in the hands of local authorities, to buy the most appropraite and cost-effective care for them. His plan, which became the bill, required all local authorities to assess the individual care needs of everyone in their areas and draw up a plan for them.

It would have unleashed huge repressed demand for services, but as the year progressed, John Major, Mrs Thatcher's new chancellor, was making it increasingly clear that there would be no new money for anything next year. Mrs Thatcher had never liked the scheme because it gave too much power to local authorities. The treasury thought it looked far too open-ended. Kenneth Clarke had always wanted the money and control to be given to health authorities, not local authorities. And he wanted to divert whatever money he could get from the treasury into easing the problems of the NHS over the next year. Nor did he want to face vigorous complaints next year that the new community care scheme was underfunded.

But it was the single most popular piece of legislation during this session. The opposition largely applauded it – though it was concerned that not enough money would be put into the scheme. All the major influential organisations and charities concerned with welfare of the old and handicapped welcomed it with amazed delight. The trades unions supported it. But with a serious financial squeeze planned for next year's spending round, the scheme had too few supporters in the cabinet, and notably lacked the support of the leader herself. It was allowed to trundle through the Commons, only to be killed off almost immediately afterwards. Hardly was the ink dry on the royal assent when, in July, Kenneth Clarke announced to the House of Commons that the scheme would be postponed until 1993, after the next election – which effectively amounts, most observers feel, to the end of it altogether.

One of the strangest pieces of legislation this session also came from the department of health. The long delayed human fertilisation and embryology bill was reluctantly brought before parliament following passionate debates over many years on a parcel of issues raised in private members' bills. Embryo research, abortion, and related matters come up session after session but they have never had a chance of reaching a fair vote, let alone the statute book, without the government granting parliamentary time.

Long ago a promise was wrung out of the government that there would be a bill. But because of the passions raised and the complexity of the issue the government had been deeply unwilling to tangle with it – and it was uncertain how to proceed without running into inordinate political trouble on a subject offering little political gain.

Finally, in an odd and unique compromise, a bill was produced with alternative clauses, either to allow, or to ban, embryo research. The government itself took no sides on the matter. The bill was drafted to allow amendments on abortion, without the bill itself actually mentioning abortion.

The Warnock committee's report had lain on the shelf since 1984, leaving the doctors who worked in the field operating in a legal vacuum. Warnock had recommended that research should be allowed on embryos up to fourteen days after conception. A voluntary licensing authority had been set up to supervise all work on embryos. The bill proposed that if embryo research were to be allowed, the voluntary authority should become statutory, forcing all doctors and scientists to operate with a licence, within agreed rules. Long ago the cross-party battle lines had been drawn up, ever since Enoch Powell first tried to end research with a private member's bill. On one side were those, led mainly by Roman Catholics, fundamentalist Christians and orthodox Jews, who believed the killing of embryos was a desecration of human life. They argued that all human life is sacred from the moment of conception. They said that the fourteen-day cut-off point was arbitrary, and as soon as researchers wanted longer, they would be re-applying to have the time extended. Others supported them through fear of the scientific horrors that could be unleashed upon the world by interference with human genes. Where might such research lead? Cloning of a super-race? Damage to the human gene pool itself?

On the other side stood most of the medical profession, the scientific establishment, the Archbishop of York, organisations representing the one in ten couples who are infertile, plus organisations representing sufferers of hereditary diseases, pressing for more research to prevent the birth of children with dreadful handicaps.

The debate was fierce and emotional. Some MPs, like Dafydd Wigley and Peter Thurnham, both parents of children who had died of genetic diseases, told heart-rending stories in support of research that could prevent such tragedy in future. The anti-researchers wheeled handicapped people outside parliament who said they were glad to be alive even if disabled, and research would have meant they would never have been given a chance to live.

Doctors such as Robert Edwards and Robert Winston, pioneers of the test tube baby technique, said that without further research the whole programme would end. It would mean no hope for the childless or for those families carrying genes for diseases such as muscular dystrophy or haemophilia. The research would still be carried out, genetic diseases would, quite soon, be eradicable, but Britain, now leading the world, would lose out.

Mrs Thatcher, Kenneth Clarke and Virginia Bottomley all made their support for research known. First the House of Lords, then finally, on 23 April, the House of Commons, gave a decisive vote in favour of allowing research up to fourteen days of gestation. On a free vote, 364 MPs voted in favour, 193 against.

Doctors Robert Edwards and Robert Winston, committed to the continuation of embryo research.

Abortion was linked to the issue in the minds of anti-abortionists. If it was legal to conduct research only up to fourteen days on an embryo outside the womb, why was it legal to kill a foetus at twenty-eight weeks in the womb? Since David Steel's 1967 abortion act, there have been 18 private members' bills attempting to reduce the time limit. They failed, argued the anti-abortionists, simply because there was never parliamentary time given to bring the matter to the vote.

There was plainly concern among MPs that abortion rates were rising. At the same time, the date at which babies could survive after birth had been reduced through medical advance to about twenty-five weeks. The Commons debate lasted eight hours, followed by a complex procedural maze of votes lasting two and a half hours, stretching out into the early hours of the morning of 24 April. MPs had the chance to vote for various options ranging from an eighteen-week to a twenty-eight week limit. They opted for twenty-four weeks, with exceptions permitted, up to birth, for serious abnormalities or risks to the mother's health. These exemption clauses have had the overall effect of greatly liberalising rather than limiting the law. Many of those likely to have late abortions are those in whom serious abnormality is not discovered until late on in pregnancy. Under the old law, they would have been refused the chance of an abortion.

Over recent years, MPs have been more strongly lobbied on this issue than any other. Their mail bags have been weighed down with embryo and abortion letters and postcards. There have been crude attempts to intimidate those in marginal constituencies. Some churches actually asked parishioners to write to their MPs as part of a Lenten penance. In the end, many MPs said they had been angered and offended by these tactics. The worst, they felt, was a life-size plastic foetus sent to every MP just before the debate, which shocked many. The moral fervour had reached such a pitch that many MPs, indifferent to the issue, simply wanted the debate over and done with, once and for all.

The losers were devastated, doubly so as they had been confident of success. They said some MPs had promised their votes, then reneged at the last moment. They protested later that, in the early hours of the morning, befuddled MPs didn't understand the final complex clauses in which they voted to allow a wide range of exemptions from the twenty-four week rule, and had mistakenly liberalised a law they meant to tighten. However, it has dealt with the issue for the rest of this parliament, although campaigners moved by moral conviction will undoubtedly feel duty bound to try and try again to tighten the laws in the future.

For a government often given to moral pronouncements, with plentiful speeches exhorting people to higher moral values, there has been markedly little attempt in the last decade to incorporate any of this into legislation. But during the year there were increasing calls for something to be done about the growing numbers of divorced and abandoned mothers – who now totalled 1.2 million. In July, Mrs Thatcher announced that the government was to bring in powers to tax errant fathers at source. There will be a formula to make them pay realistic sums, about £50 a week. Such a measure may go some way to covering the government's embarrassment over the disclosure, also in July, that income inequality, between rich and poor, was greater than at any time since the war.

Politically though, poverty, homelessness and the lack of community care are far less dangerous to the government than a crisis in the NHS. The smooth and successful introduction of the NHS changes from next April is likely to take priority in distribution of treasury money over everything else in the social field. And yet, before the next election, all that the government can hope for from the reorganised NHS is for there to be no major problems. Whatever benefits may accrue from the plan could not start to show themselves until well after the next election, and perhaps not until far beyond that. If the scheme turns out to be a major improvement on the old NHS, then it will have been a far-sighted reform, of the kind governments are accused of not undertaking often enough. But if its introduction causes chaos in the next year leading up to an election, then many on the government benches may ask themselves why it was ever embarked on, with such a slender political up-side and a huge risk of serious political trouble.

AMERICA *in* *the* BUSH ERA

Bush had every reason to look abroad

in 1990. Power bases were shifting in

Eastern Europe and Central America and,

besides, at home he faced a nation of

disgruntled lipreaders

Gavin Esler

The colonel laughed because the tanks fell on the floor, followed by the armoured personnel carriers and artillery. He was joined by half a dozen others, all colonels, all in battle fatigues, who watched as an entire Soviet armoured division was upset by clumsiness and spilled from its box across the tiles.

After a few minutes, the fun over, the stiff fingers of the US army's best and brightest began picking up the plastic models, laying them out painstakingly across a table top according to the dispositions of Soviet forces which they were learning from the latest military intelligence reports.

US army officers thought worthy of the fast track are enrolled in the tactical commanders' development programme where they learn how to fight in the Pentagon's latest nightmares. Invariably, their 'next war' is a computer-simulated re-run of the cold war apocalypse with Soviet tanks thrusting across a battlefield which looks like the plains of northern Germany. They learn to co-ordinate all the assets of a modern general – tanks, artillery, infantry, air support – then, as the course ends, they move on to the real thing, or as near to war as is possible without its casualties.

In the heat of California's Mojave desert the

commanders and their troops fight battle exercises against what the Pentagon calls 'the best equipped Soviet regiment in the world' – Americans who play the enemy role, pseudo-Soviets who use Warsaw Pact tactics and dress themselves and their vehicles to look like the communist aggressor.

This was the American military throughout 1990. Yet it proved that if perestroika was painfully slow in the Pentagon, all the old cold war games seemed at last part of America's past not its future. 'We teach emerging Soviet tactics here,' a course instructor said candidly. 'But right now, what with all the changes, we don't

exactly know what they are.'

As the Warsaw Pact fell apart, the officers on the training programme were like generals through the ages – fighting the last war, not the next. They roared their tanks round the Californian desert, training for an unlikely war against an increasingly unreliable Soviet enemy, when suddenly a Middle East leader most Americans had never heard of threatened Armageddon in a real desert battlefield.

Saddam Hussein's invasion of Kuwait was George Bush's Pearl Harbor, a single event which galvanised the first post-cold war White House, the nation and, under American leadership, much of the world, into

A camel observes – unruffled – a US tank taking position in the Saudi desert.

diplomatic, economic and military mobilisation. Iraq's aggression promised to be the defining event of the Bush presidency, helping re-shape America's changing relationship with Europe, the Soviet Union, Japan, the Arab world and the United Nations. It led to the biggest military intervention by the United States since Vietnam, the most rapid build-up since Korea and, according to Mr Bush, one of the most significant foreign commitments since the Second World War. It also produced the boldest initiatives from a habitually cautious president, a man for whom the word 'prudent' is the highest praise, when he set American terms as nothing less than complete Iraqi withdrawal from Kuwait.

Within the course of nine months George Bush had committed US troops to three military actions: the small war in Panama, the sideshow in Liberia, and the potentially major conflict in Iraq. He had confronted the Democrats over the biggest budget deficit ever, faced the prospect of oil-price shock boosting inflation and provoking an economic recession, and yet like his hero, Theodore Roosevelt, Bush spoke softly while carrying – and using – a big stick.

'He's like a Clint Eastwood gunslinger,' a former senior Reagan administration official told the BBC. 'He doesn't say very much, but when he feels he has to act, however tough it may be, Bush does whatever it takes.'

Whatever it takes is the hallmark of George Bush's career.

The Texan president – recalling the Alamo – spoke of drawing a 'line in the sand' which Saddam Hussein crossed at his peril. George Bush was the reluctant cowboy muttering that a president had to do what a president had to do. And that, in 1990, the year of the foreign policy presidency, meant following ever so carefully in the footsteps of two predecessors who had their political careers gunned down by the men in black. Both the Carter and Reagan presidencies were spoiled by adventures in the Gulf, the Tehran hostage crisis and Iran-Contra affairs. Both provided George Bush with lessons on how not to move through the Middle East minefield.

From the start, Bush's careful diplomacy produced a unanimous vote in the United Nations Security Council against Iraq's annexation of Kuwait. That mandate, backed even by China and the Soviet Union in a diplomatic 'peace dividend' at the end of the cold war, allowed Bush great freedom to act as a global policeman with the United Nations' blessing, pushing US troops into Saudi Arabia at such a pace that one massive transport aircraft landed every ten minutes. It also helped rebuild America's floundering sense of purpose and worth in a changing world, having lost a Soviet enemy without discovering an alternative role.

Once Iraq had a chokehold on oil supplies and prices, the world looked to Washington – not Tokyo or Berlin and certainly not to Moscow – for leadership in the Gulf crisis. Saddam Hussein had fired a pistol shot at a concert, electrifying and energising the United States in a year in which peace, not war, had otherwise dominated the American agenda.

Spring 1990, and on the senate floor the much-respected chairman of the armed services committee rises to speak. Democratic senator Sam Nunn, reflecting on the changes in the Soviet Union, says there appears to be a 'threat blank' at the heart of American defence policy. No one knows who the enemy is because the cold war is finished. That has led to a 'strategy blank' in the Pentagon and, by implication, a leadership blank in the White House. George Bush, the man who was once characterised as a political 'wimp', was standing on the sidelines of history while Marxism unravelled, lacking a vision for the future of the nation, the most damnable presidential myopia.

For more than forty years the guiding star of US foreign policy had been the mission to 'contain' communism, yet in 1990 the idea of a Kremlin-directed world conspiracy to encircle the United States with hostile powers and overthrow capitalism became as relevant to political decision-making as the Flat Earth Society. 'How can Americans feel threatened,' one former Reagan defence adviser, Dr Lawrence Korb, asked, 'by a Soviet Union in which most citizens cannot even find enough sugar for their tea?'

Historically, 'containment' found its clearest expression in a penetrating 1947 analysis of Soviet aims in an essay by George Kennan, a state department expert. Kennan took Marxist dogma at face value: the supposedly eternal conflict between capitalism and communism, with communism at length triumphing. Since Soviet expansion could appear anywhere, Kennan argued, it had to be countered everywhere. That meant the arsenal of democracy cranked into life in dirty wars over four decades involving every continent on earth with the possible exception of Antarctica: Korea and Vietnam; the crisis over Cuba or Berlin; interventions either directly or through surrogates in Chile; Nicaragua; Afghanistan and Angola; the Middle East.

One result was that every American foreign policy initiative, from foreign aid and the Peace Corps to cultural programmes, scholarships for foreign intellectuals and military assistance, was at least in part driven by the need to contain communism.

The United States had carved out for itself the role of global policeman and salesman of democracy, promoting American values and interests everywhere on earth. But in 1990 the triumph of the values left the advancing of American interests a more naked and difficult fight – not against the Soviet Union, the new sick man of Europe, but on trade and economic expansion with increasingly prosperous and assertive allies in Europe and the Far East. The prospect was not of battlefield commanders countering Soviet tanks, but of businessmen and farmers defending against a Japanese and European economic push into the American heartland.

Then arose Saddam Hussein, a new devil, a new challenge of the kind America found easy to understand. American values – rule of law, protection of the weak from the strong – were at one with the more brutal American interest of taking a dictator's hands off the jugular of world oil supplies. And with the Soviet Union apparently playing a positive role at the United Nations, it seemed the old second world war alliance embracing Washington, Moscow, London and Paris might be back in business, standing up to an expansionist and ruthless dictator, truly pulling a new world from the ashes of the cold war.

George Herbert Walker Bush, forty-first president of the United States, wakes early, strides into the Oval Office for his morning intelligence briefing. His White House is, by the standards of the Reagan administration, competently if not charismatically run. Unlike Reagan, Bush is alert, the master of detail. He runs, hunts, fishes, plays golf, drives his own power boat. It is an action man presidency in which Bush runs his own foreign policy more firmly from the White House than any president since Richard Nixon.

His White House does not leak as much or as destructively as the competing baronies which exploited Ronald Reagan's managerial weakness. Bush prizes loyalty, using a Rolodex file with, it is rumoured, the telephone numbers of 6,000 'close friends', including world leaders, to push forward his policies. The Bush telephone has replaced the Reagan megaphone.

Bush began 1990 with two big allies: popularity and luck. Some 70 per cent of the electorate told opinion pollsters they thought he was doing a good job, an important power resource in the president's frequent struggles with congress. The paradox arose when as many as two-thirds of those same voters said the country was 'on the wrong track', suggesting that the

Bush popularity was fragile, a surge of affection for the friendly, open style – a kind of 'preppinesse oblige' – of a man who was not Ronald Reagan but a recognition that in the end, 'not being Ronald Reagan' might not be good enough.

The lucky president found the foreign policy objectives of every administration since Harry Truman's tumbling into his welcoming lap. Communism was no longer being contained, it rolled over and died. The CIA reported that the Soviet Union's control over Eastern Europe was lost for the foreseeable future, an irreversible change in the balance of world power. Regional conflicts from Nicaragua to Angola and Korea found the superpowers in agreement not argument. Germany, unified – astonishingly, within NATO – Czechoslovakia, Poland, Hungary, even Romania and Bulgaria, appeared on some kind of road to democracy. How the ghosts of Truman, Eisenhower, Kennedy and Johnson must have envied George Bush. And yet . . . did he achieve any of it? George was there, but did he do it?

In Panama, he did.

The former Panamanian dictator Colonel Omar Torrijos Herrera used to say that the United States was like a monkey on a chain – you could play with the monkey, but never pull the chain. His successor, General Manuel Antonio Noriega, repeatedly pulled the chain, and just before Christmas 1989 the monkey reacted. Relatively minor harassment of US military personnel in Panama had become a potential political timebomb for Bush, still labouring under the 'wimp' label. Would he ever be tough enough on the world stage?

Panama – like Ronald Reagan's invasion of the tiny Caribbean island of Grenada – showed the new commander-in-chief in command, burying the 'wimp factor' for ever. Despite civilian casualties and the fact it took far longer to subdue Noriega than the Pentagon first supposed, Panama was a rite of passage in which George Bush first exercised the real power of the presidency.

Score one for Bush – though Panama may yet return to haunt him when Noriega takes the stand in his 1991 Miami trial and describes two decades of co-operation between his intelligence officers and the CIA, which George Bush once controlled.

Within two months of Noriega's fall, Bush had a second success in Central America. Nicaragua's Sandinista regime was overwhelmingly rejected by the country's voters. After a decade of American subversion,

'As I look around this hemisphere at Panama, Nicaragua and Cuba it seems to me it is two down and one to go. Noriega is history and now so is Ortega.'
Senator Robert Dole on Daniel Ortega's defeat in the Nicaraguan elections

CIA dirty tricks, Oliver North's crude attempts illegally to fund the Contra guerrillas, and an economic embargo – all in the name of 'containment' – came that most subversive event, a fair election. The people of Nicaragua, tired of civil war, the military draft and the incompetent handling of their economy, threw out one of the world's most charismatic leftists, Daniel Ortega, and elected Violeta Chamorro, Nicaragua's housewife-superstar, at the head of a ramshackle UNO coalition. After all Nicaragua's agonies – and Washington's decade-long fixation with this tiny country – the Sandinistas' end came with less a bang than a whimper.

Nicaragua's president, Daniel Ortega, carefree and riding high before his fall from power.

Score two for Bush? Well, he may have wished it were so, but the administration did very little to bring about Chamorro's victory. The Nicaraguan people – like those of Eastern Europe – provided Bush with a success, not the other way round. Apparently convinced by the CIA's assessments that the Sandinistas were going to win, Republicans had begun discounting Nicaragua's election weeks before it took place. Until the result.

To make a Latin American hat-trick in 1990, the administration turned its attention to someone even more difficult than Noriega, and even more dangerous than Ortega: Fidel Castro. Once the darling of the left, Castro had been in power for more than thirty years, a unique revolutionary leader of a genuinely popular insurrection, yet by 1990 his was a revolution in menopause. As multi-party democracy swept Eastern Europe and Latin America, the grey-bearded Castro looked out of place and out of time in his green battle fatigues, repeating variations on the old slogans like some kind of Marxist ancient mariner. 'Socialism or death,' he bellowed, but as the economy weakened and the

Honeckers and Ortegas fell from power, Castro seemed to be spelling out less an alternative for Cuba than for himself. George Bush would, of course, like Castro as a large bearded trophy on the Oval Office wall. But rolling back communism in a country where it was imported after a home-grown revolution rather than – as in Eastern Europe – by the invading Red Army, proved a difficult task.

'The day of the dictator is over,' Bush cheered, yet he repeatedly proved more generous with his mouth than his wallet to the new democracies. There was no Marshall plan for Eastern Europe; no most favoured nation trading status or cash aid for Moscow, and the major recipients of US foreign aid in 1990 remained stalwarts of containment like Israel, Egypt and Pakistan. Panama received crumbs from the aid table, and Nicaragua fared just as badly. Republicans proved more eager to back the Contra war than the Chamorro peace. 'Our attitude is simple,' one astute Washington political commentator said, describing the lack of aid to fledgling democracies. 'We say to these countries: "So, you've thrown off the dictators now? Great! Have a nice day!"'

It is early June, and Mikhail Gorbachev has been persuaded to visit the president's country retreat at Camp David. George Bush wanted Gorbachev to stay at his family home on the ocean in Maine, to relax and fish. Other foreign leaders had been enticed to shirt-sleeve summits, but Gorbachev, bedevilled by domestic problems, and an unlikely fishing companion said, no, Camp David is far enough.

A hot day, blue skies, sun glinting from the White House. On the freshly-cut lawn Marine One sits waiting. The two most powerful men in the world stride towards the helicopter, cheerful, relaxed. The summit has gone well, with major agreements on chemical and strategic nuclear weapons in the bag, and more on the way. Suddenly, another figure walks out, a man in the uniform of a US air force major, also with a place on the helicopter. Strapped to his wrist is a fat attaché case known as 'the football' containing all the codes necessary for George Bush to launch a nuclear strike against the Soviet Union, should, during the course of his flight, he find Gorbachev's company unbearable.

It is the image of 1990 in Washington and a metaphor for superpower relations: two nations struggling to move from outright hostility towards something which might become friendship – but not yet.

In the words of US defence secretary Dick Cheney,

it was not wise to give away the defence overcoat 'just because it is the first warm day of January'. Even so, there were the beginnings of a vision of the world after containment – no grand plan, just the skeleton of a 'Bush doctrine' on America's new role.

Firstly, America must stay involved as well as alert, no sudden cashing in for a 'peace dividend' and no return to isolationism or a fortress America. Iraq proved there were still bears in the woods, even if they were not of the Russian variety. Secondly, the nations of Europe and elsewhere have the right to choose their own forms of government and their own systems of alliances. And finally, that meant that the German question, for the third time this century, dominated world politics and the White House. In fact, the peaceful unification of Germany within NATO was the central Bush ambition of 1990 – a recognition that in a sense, Germany *was* NATO: that's where the troops were; that's where the border was; and that was where the colonels in the Californian desert still planned to fight their 'next war', before Saddam Hussein.

As the Bush doctrine stumbled into words in a White House where oratory was not a high political skill, the president played a canny hand. He tried to re-invent Europe without humiliating the Soviet Union or irritating his NATO allies. He cultivated the West German chancellor Helmut Kohl, publicly praising and frequently consulting him, creating a new 'special relationship' which rivalled but did not eclipse that supposedly existing between Washington and London for decades.

The biggest headache was in deciding how tough to be with Mikhail Gorbachev. The Soviet leader came to the Washington summit a beleaguered visionary, suffering miseries of biblical proportions, tormented by demons like Boris Yeltsin, military conservatives and secessionist republics, economic disaster, political collapse.

But, as American right-wingers endlessly pointed out, like Orwell's perverse politics in the novel *1984*, for Gorbachev 'weakness was strength'. Domestic calamities put his very survival at risk, and for Bush the question was whether he should push hard for concessions on those issues which divided the superpowers – notably arms control, Lithuania, and Germany – or whether he should soften because otherwise he might provoke a Kremlin backlash, plunging superpower relations back into the diplomatic dark ages. And that could put some kind of Stalinist monster back in the Kremlin, or the erratic Boris Yeltsin or, even worse, provoke anarchy and instability in a country with a mighty nuclear arsenal.

Pragmatists argued there was a risk of producing a Weimar Russia. Bush, like the victorious allies after the first world war who wanted to squeeze Germany till the pips squeaked, might crush Gorbachev and create a sense of grievance so strong that, as with Hitler's rise in Weimar Germany, the result would be some ultra-nationalist Russian leader prepared to risk war as a means of restoring national dignity. Ideologues on the Republican right took precisely the opposite view, believing every Soviet concession had been gained by America standing firm, giving nothing.

Bush sided firmly with the pragmatists.

Former supreme allied commander Europe and Reagan secretary of state, General Al Haig, referring to one of the more comic Bush moments of the year – the president's decision to ban broccoli from White House menus because his mother forced him to eat it as a child – told the BBC: 'I suppose you could say Bush now has a balanced policy. Tough on broccoli, soft on the Soviets.'

Yet Haig's comment revealed more about the weakness of the far right than the White House. Publicly, Bush refused to allow that his judgment was ever clouded by wishing to help Gorbachev stay in power, but if Gorbachev were to fall, how could Bush escape blame? The most obvious parallel was with China, which turned communist in 1949, leading to a decade of debate in the United States about 'who lost China'. For Bush, the question 'Who lost Gorby?' could destroy the lucky presidency. His best re-election card for 1992, foreign policy competence, would disintegrate. The left would say he gave too little, the right that he gave too much.

But the Bush concessions were slow and halting. At the NATO summit he refused to commit NATO to 'no first use' of nuclear weapons, though he did describe them as 'truly weapons of last resort'. In practice, it was a distinction without a difference, but diplomatically it proved a significant coup. NATO fell into line, and Gorbachev soon agreed to German unification within the western alliance.

Two weeks later at the Houston economic summit the world's seven richest capitalist countries fudged the question of aid to the Soviet Union. On one side, Germany offered $3 billion in credit guarantees. France supported a $20 billion cash fund. On the other, Britain thought it all a waste of money. The US was even more sceptical, and Japan downright hostile – what about our

Kuril Islands, occupied by the Soviets since 1945? The final communiqué promised a 'study' of Soviet needs, but recognised a simple yet highly significant political fact. Each country had already decided to go its own way on aid to the USSR, something quite unthinkable even five years ago, and a landmark for the 1990s.

The lesson of this 1990 epidemic of summitry was that Washington's leadership of NATO's military doctrine remained unchallenged, but the purely military significance of NATO had rapidly diminished. On questions of economic and political leadership, like Soviet aid, America had influence but far from absolute

George Bush at the Pentagon for a high-level briefing on the Gulf crisis.

power, and even that limited power may shrink if the US economy continues to weaken.

In Houston, prime minister Margaret Thatcher, leader of a nation forced to manage its own economic, military and political decline over the past two generations, graphically summed up the new world after containment. There were now three great economic systems, she casually observed: those built around the dollar, the yen and the Deutschmark. Two visions of political reality – communist and capitalist – had been replaced by three competing capitalist blocs, signalling new dangers as well as opportunities.

America's founding fathers were possessed of two firm political beliefs: that mankind contains such wickedness that there must be checks and balances to prevent too much power accruing in the hands of potential despots, and that it was possible to create a near-perfect political machine – a constitution – by which such checks and balances could lead to the wise government of their new nation.

In 1990 this clever separation of powers led to an extraordinary game of pass the political parcel with an obscenity so dreadful it was referred to merely by the euphemism 'the T word' – taxes.

Congressional Democrats and the Bush administration recognised that, despite George Bush's only memorable campaign slogan, 'Read my lips – no new taxes', the US economy was in such difficulty that even the T word might have to re-enter polite political conversation. The trick would be to ensure that the other side ended up taking the political blame for something almost everyone, in differing degrees, thought necessary.

Throughout the year, a lot of men in smart suits made the short trip up Pennsylvania Avenue from Capitol Hill to the White House to discuss the economy with the president. Then a lot of men in smart suits from the Bush administration made the trip back down Pennsylvania Avenue to continue their conversations with respected members of congress. The constitutional separation of powers allowed everyone to say they were acting in the best interests of the nation, setting aside party interests, open agenda, difficult decisions, nettles to be grasped . . . blah, blah, blah.

Taxes, like nuclear bombs, were truly weapons of last resort, yet absolutely necessary if Bush wanted to create his 'kinder, gentler America,' improving the environment, education and roads, and paying for a manned mission to Mars which he hoped would capture the imagination of a generation of young Americans and turn them towards science.

The president, though he would never say it so bluntly, wanted the Mars mission to help win the high technology race with Japan and Europe in the 1990s the way the Apollo programme to put a man on the Moon had helped win the space race with the Soviet Union in the 1960s. Yet the Mars mission had a thirty-year time-table, not Apollo's ten years. It would fire the imagina-tion of the nation's young scientists right through to middle age – which might give the deficit-ridden and bureaucratically inert government time to work out how to pay the bills.

Such commitments and budget problems on earth and beyond forced the president to soften his 'no new taxes' pledge, saying that 'tax revenue increases' were now necessary, though details remained vague. 'Read my lips,' one comedian said of Bush. 'I lied.'

The economist John Kenneth Galbraith was equally amused. 'Tax reform,' Galbraith wrote of the economic philosophy behind the Reagan tax-cutting spree and Bush's original commitment to no new taxes, 'was made urgent because our rich had not been work-ing because they had too little income and our poor because they had too much.' The implications of that delicious paradox never took hold within the White House, but George Bush was left staring at the 'T word' if he had any hope of achieving even part of his list of domestic priorities.

The crisis over Iraq hid these more intractable domestic difficulties, and it proved easier to create a kinder gentler NATO than pay for a kinder gentler America.

In the Bush presidency there are still beggars and homeless just a few blocks away from the White House, the tired, poor, huddled masses yearning for a bit of loose change. There are still nightly gun battles in American cities between crack dealers using weapons most third world armies would be lucky to possess. The average life expectancy of a black man in Harlem is less than that of a Bengali in Bangladesh, and if you happen to be young, black and male in New York city, the likeliest cause of death is homicide. George Bush's kinder, gentler America so far is only a state of the heart.

It was hardly surprising therefore that in 1990 George Bush – like his Soviet counterpart – found in foreign affairs an escape from domestic difficulties. If 'the vision thing' often remained murky, Saddam Hussein helped point the way. 'The issue of Soviet–American relations,' the architect of containment

'Arrows have been flying, back, front, sideways. But that is what I get paid for.'
President Bush after reneging on his 'read my lips, no new taxes' campaign pledge

George Kennan wrote in his 1947 article (though one could just as easily substitute Japanese–American, European–American or Iraqi–American relations), 'is in essence a test of the overall worth of the United States as a nation among nations. To avoid destruction the United States need only measure up to its own best traditions and prove itself worthy of preservation as a great nation.'

If Kennan is correct, then the United States should be less distressed by new challenges to American interests, except (as in the Middle East) where the challenge is violent and the interests are both international and vital. Instead it should merely enjoy the triumph of American values – even if the phrase is impertinent, suggesting a western tradition owing more to Jefferson than Plato or Aristotle.

The implication is that the 1990s might mean the best of America: a renewed enthusiasm for a changing world role; a restless energy; an international commitment to succeed not just as the salesmen of American goods but also of freedom and democracy. Or it might foretell the worst in America: another lapse at the end of a war into introspection; disgust with former allies; suspicion of others' economic growth; protectionism, envy and isolation.

The decision largely rests with George Bush, by instinct and training an internationalist. From the White House lawn, he has a humbling view. He can see monuments to two of his greatest predecessors, George Washington and Abraham Lincoln, both inspirational war leaders, both constructing new Americas from confusion and conflict. As he sits in the Oval Office pondering the months ahead, George Bush may, if the world is lucky, never have a monument dedicated to him as a president who rose to the challenge of America under the threat of destruction. In whatever way the Gulf crisis is finally resolved, the underlying challenges are those of a fragile peace, less glamorous than those of the cold war, but no less arduous and no less worth the struggle.

SOUTH AFRICA
at the
CROSSROADS

South Africa's president, F. W. de Klerk,

has chosen danger now rather than

catastrophe later by opening negotiations

on power-sharing with the ANC

David Dimbleby

For forty years, successive National party governments have tried to force South Africa into a mould which it cannot fit. The separation of different groups in South Africa would have allowed five million whites to retain 87 per cent of South Africa, and to govern themselves with a clear conscience in the belief that the political demands of all other races could be met in their own homelands. The reality, as finally became clear even to the National party, was that the attempt was futile and its effects devastating. It was based on a series of fictions which could not be passed off as fact; in particular the belief that over 30 million blacks could be persuaded that it was right for whites to own most of the country and its wealth while they, increasingly in demand to work in factories, service industries and businesses in white areas, could be treated as guest workers, as foreigners, whose political and national loyalties were diverted elsewhere.

A majority of whites seemed to believe this scheme was practical though they accepted that it would take time to achieve. They were aggrieved by the onslaught on South Africa from overseas, where moral outrage at the methods used to implement apartheid precluded serious consideration of the proposed political structure. Even now, the National party makes no apology for having attempted to introduce apartheid, shows no sign of guilt at the damage, and does not admit to political error in leading its supporters up a cul-de-sac. On the contrary, the interpretation it puts on de Klerk's decision to abandon apartheid and negotiate the sharing of power is that it is the natural outcome of a serious attempt to reconcile the different racial groups of South Africa which regrettably failed.

The National party comes to the negotiating table with no sense of 'mea culpa'. It would have done almost anything to retain white supremacy but the cost was too high. Separate schools, separate hospitals and separate housing were bureaucratically inefficient and expensive. The means used to suppress black opposition, the turbulence of the townships, the deaths and torture in detention, made South Africa unattractive to foreign investment. Sanctions, the withdrawal of foreign capital and, most damaging of all, the refusal of American banks to extend their loans, created a crisis. The government had to choose, as one commentator said, between catastrophe and danger: the catastrophe of a country facing a growing population and declining living standards, against the danger of abandoning the certainties of the past forty years in favour of a negotiated agreement on sharing power.

Forced to choose between imminent danger and catastrophe postponed, politicians prefer that which can be postponed. To his credit, President de Klerk chose danger. It was a bold and unexpected decision from a man who until then had shown no signs of kicking over the traces of National party orthodoxy. That he felt forced to do so is a sign of the scale of the catastrophe he believed his country faced. With the support of the army and the police, with laws banning political parties at will, and armed with emergency powers which, in the immortal words of the minister of law and order, had the merit that they 'allowed the arrest of more people on less evidence' the government could have carried on for several more years. But the road led nowhere. The results of the withdrawal of foreign loans were high interest rates, consistently over 20 per cent, increasing unemployment and high inflation which was hurting not just the black population but the whites as well, particularly the poorer whites who were once the bedrock of National party support.

The announcement by de Klerk in parliament in Cape Town on 2 February that the ANC was to be 'unbanned', allowed to operate as a legal political party,

'We say when the time for an idea has come, nobody can stop it. And the time for the idea of a new and just and equitable South Africa has arrived. We are going to make that come true.'
President F. W. de Klerk on his visit to London in May

Nelson Mandela freed after twenty-seven years' imprisonment leaves jail for a hero's welcome.

and the subsequent release of Nelson Mandela seemed to catch the ANC off balance. Throughout the year the political initiative was always in de Klerk's hands and the response of the ANC hesitant and confused, even as it was being offered what it had been demanding for so many years. It was bound to treat de Klerk's proposals with caution. The ANC has been subject to too much humbug, too many broken promises and too much violent suppression not to suspect that what others saw as a glimmer of hope might be a false dawn. Some still fear a sophisticated trick to fool the outside world that South Africa is mending its ways while the government procrastinates over moves to a new democratic South Africa. This suspicion of de Klerk's motives led the more radical in the ANC to urge the movement to continue its military resistance.

The notion that the ANC's army, Umkhonto we Sizwe, or MK, would ever bring the ANC to power by defeating the forces of the South African army and police has long been abandoned by more moderate members of the ANC. Mandela describes it as a purely defensive force there to protect 'our people'. Its achievements in South Africa have been neither on a large enough scale nor successful enough to discomfort the government. Relying on the Soviet Union and Eastern Europe for training and munitions, the few thousand MK members found themselves operating in difficult conditions. They were so heavily infiltrated by the South African security services and their movements were so hampered by neighbouring states which had made their peace with the apartheid regime for political reasons, that the lifespan of an ANC guerrilla penetrating South Africa was short and the damage he could inflict limited. But for many young blacks who escaped from South Africa after the violence of the mid-Seventies and Eighties a belief in the ultimate triumph of the ANC by military victory was a creed. Chris Hani, the military commander, and others in the ANC still argue that MK should be kept in reserve lest the government goes back on its word. They watch warily as Mandela and de Klerk make the first moves towards compromise.

The ANC also has problems with its young militant supporters in the townships. It is difficult to explain the full horror of the turbulent world in which these 'comrades' live. It is a state close to anarchy. The collapse of imposed order has allowed them to create a society ruled by violence, where secret kangaroo courts discipline not just their own age groups but their parents' generation too. (I have seen the proceedings of

'Friends, comrades and fellow South Africans, I greet you all in the name of peace, democracy and freedom for all. The majority of South Africans, black and white, recognise that apartheid has no future.'
Nelson Mandela, on his release from prison in February

one of these kangaroo courts. Carefully noted in an exercise book are complaints brought by aggrieved residents who no longer trust the police and want swift retribution, mostly about theft or marital squabbles. The proposed punishments ranged from fines, usually pocketed by the courts, to beatings. Occasionally a dispute is resolved: 'X promised Y to go on loving her.')

This generation is known by black teachers and leaders as the 'lost generation'. They are barely educated. The deliberate attempt by white governments to retard black education has exacted a terrible price. The schools are overcrowded, with few books, and with teachers who fear for their lives if they try to impose discipline. This inferior education is branded racist by the ANC comrades and is used to legitimise their counter-culture. Although their parents and political leaders urge them to learn what they can, however bad the schools, they adopt a tactic of constant and deliberate disruption. If the education authorities announce that schools will open on one date, the comrades announce another. When holidays are declared, the students opt to stay at school. When term starts, they announce a holiday. Day after day, week after week, teenage children are roaming the streets, some going to political meetings, others turning to crime. Their elders try to convince them that revolutionaries also need their education, but the militant young prefer the slogan of: 'Liberation now. Education later.' Those who want to sit their exams and go to universities are a sad spectacle. If they flout instructions from the comrades they face a beating or worse. At twenty or twenty-two they are sitting exams they should have passed at eighteen. With nowhere to study, no books to read, they cling to their ambitions to be doctors or lawyers or engineers, but most of them can hope for little better than their parents have achieved.

These township comrades terrorise not only their own generation and their parents' generation but frighten the ANC itself. The party line is that they are loyal and disciplined but everyone knows they are a threat. If they dislike the decisions of the ANC they have the means to oppose them. They, not the ANC, can close schools. They can enforce 'stay-aways', patrolling railway stations, bus terminals and taxi ranks to prevent township residents going to work. They, not the ANC, can barricade the streets, make petrol bombs, and stone the police.

During August and September, when supporters of Inkatha and the ANC were engaged in savage battles in several townships, I watched a prominent ANC leader trying to persuade a crowd of comrades to be patient and disciplined and refrain from attacking a Zulu hostel. Eloquently he pleaded with them not to 'create more corpses'. The response was angry mutterings of discontent and calls for the ANC to give them arms to protect their small squatter camp. The previous night they had been attacked by unknown gunmen and bodies were still lying where they had been shot. They wanted vengeance, and complained that their leadership was sitting down to negotiate peace with a government that they held responsible for the violence. The ANC knows that unless it can assuage the wrath of these comrades they will desert to more militant organisations like the PAC (Pan Africanist Congress) whose stance is more determinedly anti-white, anti-government and anti-negotiations.

Just as authoritarian regimes face the moment of greatest danger when they try to reform, so revolutionary movements face their greatest danger when they seek compromise. The ANC leadership is nervous of the reactions both of their external army, MK, and of the comrades. It is a nervousness tinged with respect, particularly for the young in the townships who have borne the brunt of the violence. The leadership living in relative comfort abroad have been victims of occasional assassination and of the misery of exile, but the township comrades have faced daily brutality. They have been subjected to harassment, to attacks with tear gas and shotguns, to the arrest, torture and indefinite detention of their leaders.

In a Soweto high school, I was talking to a group of half a dozen of these youngsters, all in their late teens or early twenties. They were explaining that, contrary to what many fearful whites say, they did not expect South Africa to be transformed overnight. 'If we go too fast we will make mistakes,' one said. But when the conversation turned to the police, two of the six asked me to feel their foreheads and hands. Embedded just under the surface of the skin were pellets of shot from confrontations with the police. Their hopes might be modest, but it would not, one felt, be easy to persuade them to accept a settlement if they thought it was a sell-out.

The ANC has its own internal problems, too, when it tries to negotiate, problems which spring from its confused aims. It would like to have presented itself as representative of all black South Africans, the liberation movement that finally brought the National party to its knees. But having failed to defeat the government militarily, it had no coherent strategy except to hope that the government would succumb to such

'I think within a matter of minutes everybody in the room understood that there was nobody in the room who had horns.'
Thabo Mbeki, ANC spokesman, after beginning talks with South Africa's white minority government

111

international pressure as the ANC could foster. When de Klerk's offer of talks was made, the ANC was already at a low ebb. The collapse of communist governments in Eastern Europe and Gorbachev's reforms in the Soviet Union had removed its principal prop. Though cash came from countries like Sweden, the education and military training of the exiles had largely depended on communist countries who believed liberation struggles would lead to communist governments or at least fellow-travelling governments in Africa. When the cold war died the ANC had nowhere to turn. The offer of talks left them wrong-footed. They were being offered a share in power by a government which held most of the good cards and could, if negotiations went badly, withdraw. No such choice was open to the ANC. It was now or never. The months since February have seen the ANC trying unsuccessfully to manoeuvre for advantage against a president who has successfully captured the high ground.

The ANC's declared aim is liberation and a multi-party democracy with guaranteed rights for individuals. But there are many within it who have other agendas. The redress of inequalities by socialism including a redistribution of wealth and extensive nationalisation is still the hope of a majority of the ANC executive. Many of them are openly members of the South African Communist party, who while propounding a new love for democracy, have a record of such slavish adherence to every twist and turn of policy in Moscow, from Stalin onwards, that the genuineness of their conversion must be treated with extreme caution.

These confusions over long-term aims allow the government great latitude. While it is true that there is a huge disparity of wealth between blacks and whites, and perhaps, as opinion polls show, a leaning towards socialism among potential black voters, it is not a foregone conclusion that a majority of newly enfranchised blacks will vote socialist or communist. Many are members of a burgeoning black middle class, who have triumphed over the adversities of apartheid, to move into professional jobs, to send their children to private schools, to build better homes. Millions more black people living in the townships aspire to the same standards of living and believe it will only be possible if South Africa, once back in the fold, becomes a developing industrial power with a high growth rate. For that they need not only the expertise of the whites but an economic structure that will entice back western investment against the supposed attractions of investment opportunities in Eastern Europe.

The government and business are campaigning to persuade sufficient numbers of new black voters that it would be better not to overthrow the present system in favour of radical changes to the structure of the economy and of society. The belief that they may be successful helps explain the sanguine acceptance of equal votes for all by a party which came to power to sustain white domination and Afrikaner interests in particular. The National party has clarified its stance during the year. It is no longer looking for the entrenchment of group rights – effectively a white blocking mechanism in the constitution. It knows this would not satisfy the Ameri-

can congress or the European Community. It is relying instead on some form of proportional representation which will give the anti-socialists enough clout to frustrate the radical plans of the ANC and allow time for the new electorate to realise the advantages of the mixed economy.

Riot police in Port Elizabeth chase demonstrators after a night of rioting which left 28 people dead across the country.

None of this will be easy. The disparity of wealth is gargantuan. It is not just in earning power, where the gap between blacks and whites doing similar work is being gradually eroded, but in every other facet of life. South Africa used to be described by whites as a bastion of 'civilised standards' compared with the rest of Africa. Now, faced with the imminent demise of apartheid and extension of the franchise, it has become orthodox to call it a 'third world' country. This ignores the advantages South Africa will have from its industrial and commercial structure, its big cities, its sophisticated financial institutions and, not least, a skilled, white professional and managerial class that would prefer not to leave; but it is an accurate description of the living conditions of a majority of black citizens. Many are crowded into squatter camps in houses made of packing cases or corrugated iron. Their children play amid the stench of rotting refuse and the grey slime of overflowing sewage. Others try to keep families clean and warm in the tiny, unheated, breeze-block houses that pass for family homes in the townships. Some live in bleak, males-only hostels, sharing rooms for thirty years, separated from their families in distant homelands.

As it prepares to share power with over 30 million blacks, the National party is praying that, once enfranchised, they will not rise up as one to redress their wrongs, but will find a host of different political voices. To encourage this they stress what to the ANC is anathema: the conflicting tribal loyalties of black people, and Indians and coloureds. At their most striking, these divisions are revealed by the militancy of the Zulu-based Inkatha movement, led by Chief Buthelezi who arouses deep-rooted suspicion in the ANC. It accuses him of being the creation of apartheid, refusing to accept that his rejection of independence for Kwa-Zulu effectively destroyed the concept of independent homelands which prime ministers from Verwoerd to Vorster had hoped to establish as the pattern for apartheid South Africa. Instead, it sees him as a proponent of Zulu nationalism and therefore of a South Africa which is not homogenously black and white.

The charge that the police, army, and even the government tolerated, connived at, or actively encouraged the violent clashes between Inkatha and the ANC, whether true or not, springs from the same suspicion: that the government will do anything it can to weaken the ANC and encourage its potential rivals. No matter that Buthelezi would be likely to command no more than a million or two votes in the new parliament, the vivid demonstration of Inkatha's power during the fighting in the townships robs the ANC of its title as sole representative of black opinion and is a chink in its armour which the government will continue to exploit. The more fractured black opinion becomes, the more

Armed Inkatha supporters chant and display their weapons as tension mounts between rival black groups.

reasonable the government's attempts to secure the rights of minorities constitutionally and thus preserve what it has always hoped to preserve, the maximum power and leverage for whites in any new constitution.

In the months since the peace process was initiated, de Klerk has shown an unflinching commitment to policies which would have been unthinkable only a year or two ago. The world of white South Africans is being turned on its head before their eyes and their reaction has been astonishment, horror, admiration or bewilderment, depending on their own prejudices and on their calculations of the outcome. For de Klerk himself there can be no turning back now, but his plan for a negotiated settlement could be derailed. This could happen in two ways. The violence unleashed by black rivalries and perhaps encouraged by sinister 'third forces', probably extreme right-wing whites, could still force his government to re-impose a general state of emergency, or even martial law. In those circumstances, however unwillingly, the ANC would be forced to leave the conference table. The other possibility, once thought the most likely, is a rebellion by whites opposed to a settlement. The Afrikaners have a tradition of bitter internecine strife and the attacks of white opponents on de Klerk, the accusations of betrayal, were to be expected.

The difficulty facing the Conservative party which represents the bulk of the government's white opponents is what to do about it. It called rather lamely for a general election on the white voters' roll, claiming that de Klerk has no mandate. It organised a rally at the Voortrekker monument at which an attendance of 100,000 was promised but only 50,000 came. It threatened to cause industrial havoc, to bring the country to a halt by leading a strike of key white workers. So far it has not happened, and white trades union members seem reluctant to take political action which would lose them wages and threaten their jobs.

Some in the Conservative party opposed what de Klerk is doing but are resigned to it: 'It's not for me,' one of them told me. 'I shall oppose it. If they wanted to do this they should have started long ago, but perhaps it will be all right for the young. Perhaps they will learn to live with it. I'm too old.'

The ballot box is the Conservatives' best hope of defeating de Klerk. An election is due in four years' time. The government wants negotiations to be completed before that date and has already said there will not be another 'whites only' election. But whites will have a chance to vote on any constitutional change

'We are speaking about black rebellion. People have not considered white reaction. I warned Mr de Klerk, if you introduce a system by which you subject the white nation to black majority rule, you are looking for trouble.'
Dr Andries Treurnicht, leader of the Conservative party in South Africa

proposed and, according to de Klerk, to veto it. If he holds a referendum on the present 'whites only' voters' roll, he will bank on winning by the de Gaulle technique – 'even if you do not like what I have done, the consequences of rejection will be worse.'

Whether the proposals are accepted or rejected, this referendum will mark a turning point for white conservatives, the moment they will have to decide whether to fight. For the government has already said that if its proposals are rejected it will not resign but resume negotiations, a step which would be interpreted by the right as a defiance of white voters. Even if the

proposals were to be accepted those whites who favour rebellion may seize the chance to try to topple the government by creating chaos. Mandela, believing that a majority of whites it likely to oppose any settlement, argues that de Klerk cannot allow white voters a veto. De Klerk appears adamant that they will be allowed their say, perhaps using the threat of a white veto to force the ANC to make more concessions on the protection of white rights than they would like.

White South Africans are not in the strictest sense colonists. They came from Europe and colonised, but most of them now have nowhere else to go. They feel as much part of the country as the Zulu or the Xhosa. This

South Africa's President, F. W. de Klerk, and Nelson Mandela start talks in Cape Town.

Clenched fist salute at the start of the Nelson Mandela concert at London's Wembley Stadium.

sense of belonging serves them well now that they are set on negotiations to share power. There is as yet no sign of panic among whites and even those opposed to de Klerk seem resigned to staying in South Africa and making the best of it. The belief that blacks will not exact revenge for the evils of the past is widespread. It has given the National party the confidence to pursue the only path which can offer South Africa the chance of a stable future. It explains the calmness with which de Klerk has embarked on a strategy none of his predecessors would have dared consider. In choosing danger now rather than catastrophe later he hopes to save his people by the very methods they thought would destroy them. The path will of course become more perilous the further he goes, but he has made an impressive start. If he succeeds it will be a personal triumph.

The POLITICS of ART

To avert the danger of becoming

'the cultural banana republic of Europe'

in the next decade, arts companies again

sought to pressure the government into

providing more funding

Andrew Burroughs

After a decade of commercialism, the Nineties promise a more philosophical mood. Mind-boggling authors Umberto Eco and Stephen Hawking dominate the best-sellers and it's hard to find a play that isn't about death or religion, or a production of *King Lear*. Often the big questions are defused rather than answered: David Hare's *Racing Demon* boils piety down to politics; Peter Greenaway's *TV Dante* interrupts the poetry with instant analysis from anthropologists. But whether as a result of the ecological crisis, or Aids, or the plight of a novelist under sentence of death for writing a book, urgent reflection about art and life is 'in'.

For the performing arts much of this urgent reflection is still about money. A third of the companies on the Arts Council's books, including some thirty theatres, start the new decade with a deficit and their directors are more likely to be consulting the ninety accountants than the nine muses. In response to financial pressure, the arts have learned to present the economic case for subsidy. Art, once a mysterious force which helped us see and feel, then a general benefit – like education – to be maintained as a public service, is now a neglected industry, slightly larger than car manufacturing, which offers unbeatable value for creating jobs, attracting tourists and regenerating depressed regions. But none of this has lifted Britain off the bottom of the European league table in public support for the arts, or prevented that most mordant critic of arts policy, Sir Roy Strong, the former director of the Victoria and Albert Museum, from declaring that Britain is becoming 'the cultural banana republic of Europe'.

Art may be mysterious, but the prime minister seems to have decided there are votes in it. Until this year, her reputation as an art-lover had been built largely on her enthusiasm for patriotic porcelain, her knack of irritating conservationists with embellish-

ments to the boudoir at Downing Street and her observation that 'a museum is something that is really rather dead'. The impression had been formed, in the minds of those annoyingly famous arts lobbyists who linked arms to defend Shakespeare's Rose Theatre, that it was not just the developers' bulldozers, but in some way Mrs Thatcher's bulldozers, which were bearing down upon them.

The new image was unveiled in January, when the Tate Gallery press office dropped hints that a VIP, indeed the VIP, would reopen the collection. This would mean fraternising with the curators of Carl André's 'Equivalent VIII', known to Tory backbenchers as 'the

'But is it art?' Mrs Thatcher at the Tate Gallery in January.

bricks' (though the piece itself had been generously offered to a Tate of the North which had apparently been built for the purpose). But a lectern in the Victorian room, emblazoned with the exhibition slogan, 'Past, Present and Future', seemed an ideal platform from which Mrs Thatcher could reveal her habit of slipping into galleries on foreign trips, and her love of Henry Moore: 'We have one in Number Ten.'

It was, perhaps, the mysterious force of this sculpture, for the prime minister's sudden embrace of art appeared rapturous. Tate director Nicholas Serota, reportedly a man of 'faint socialist conscience', was praised for his 'genius', and Mrs Thatcher declared: 'Always, but always, it is not enough to conserve the heritage, we have to enlarge it before we pass it on.' New artists must be looked after, she went on, and new paintings bought, to make London the artistic capital of Europe. This must have sounded to Mr Serota very like a promise to expand galleries' purchasing grants, frozen in 1985 (since which time art prices have risen by 400 per cent). Downing Street officials assured me it was nothing of the kind.

Mrs Thatcher continued her reassurance of the art world with an account of her childhood love of Pieter Bruegel the Elder, this possibly made less reassuring by her unusual pronunciation of the name, as 'Broil'. Mr Serota may have reflected that, only weeks before, the last privately-owned Bruegel landscape likely to come on the market had gone under the hammer at Sotheby's for £860,000, with no British gallery able to make so much as a bid. In the absence of new pictures to hang, Mrs Thatcher was invited to see the 'rehang', a term she baulked at, suggestive as it is of a particularly morbid public spectacle from the seventeenth century. She preferred to call it a 'redisplay, a rejuvenation'. Arts reporters, suspecting that they were witnessing not a 'rejuvenation' but merely a 'rehang' of government policy, ambushed her in the modern sculpture hall, and put the unkindest question they could think of – what did she think of abstract sculpture?

Some were less reassured than others. As the former director of a business sponsorship foundation, and a former Conservative councillor, the Arts Council secretary-general, Luke Rittner, had once been seen as a government poodle. During his tenure, the council, which has controlled public funds for the arts for forty years, had been accused of changing sides – of presenting the government's case to the artists, instead of the artists' case to the government. But it was in protest at government interference that he suddenly resigned in

March, becoming an instant hero of the arts lobby.

Mr Rittner's last new conference was reminiscent of Basil Fawlty and the Germans. He was there to explain the government's plans, but had been told: 'Don't mention the resignation!' He had seemed on safe enough ground with a definition of post-war arts policy. It was to keep the politicians at arm's length from artistic decisions – allowing the politicians to decide how much was spent, but leaving the arts profes-sionals to decide where it was spent. Without the arm's length principle (and there weren't many of those in Europe, he suggested) arts and politics became blurred, and artistic directors were undermined. Then he was asked whether he thought government plans would threaten this tradition: 'You are coming perilously close to asking me about . . . my resignation.'

So, what were these dire proposals? Mr Rittner had only referred darkly to the arts minister, Richard Luce, going 'beyond Wilding'. This was an allusion, not to New York hoodlums, but to the innocuous Wilding report on how regional arts organisations should relate to London. The government had unexpectedly seized on this as an excuse for the biggest shake-up of the Arts Council in its history. Most of its 160 companies and its cash would be devolved to new regional boards. The council was supposed to keep its clout, but for Mr Rittner, since the politicians were imposing these changes on the professionals, the arm's length principle had been violated. In an oblique tribute, *The Guardian*, which had greeted his arrival at the council as another step towards philistinism, now greeted his departure as another step towards philistinism.

No one at the Arts Council had expected a coup from Mr Luce. This quiet foreign office hand had sur-vived unnoticed through half a decade of reshuffles and, modestly claiming no expertise in the arts, had kept out of the crossfire between the council and the treasury. True, he had set a Thatcherite tone with his call for the arts to be weaned away from the 'welfare state mentality', but he had just emerged triumphantly from the 1990 budget having secured a 12 per cent increase for the arts, the best deal for a decade. Mr Luce wasn't exactly beating the tom-toms, but he appeared to be happily going native. In reality, he had had a bruising time of it. He had assumed that even the trea-sury would be concerned for the nation's 'treasures'. However, when it heard his stories of underfunding and leaking museum roofs, he found he had embarked on a Herculean task of persuasion, which, rumour had it, he had only accomplished after threatening to resign.

How galling then, having nailed his own colours to the mast, to see the so called 'flagship' companies hoisting the Jolly Roger. The English National Opera, which had followed his precepts on the need for commercial marketing with steamy poster campaigns, now declared it would be 'budgeting for a deficit' – a phrase calculated to appal Mr Luce. It was a familiar tactic: maintain artistic standards consistent with your charter and your reputation (rave reviews), and seat prices your target audience can afford (full houses), and, if you still end up in debt, say it must be the government's fault. The Royal Opera House followed suit with double the deficit, and the last straw came with headlines announcing the Royal Shakespeare Company's decision to close its London theatres for a third of the year to save money. The very people whose case Mr Luce had pleaded so eloquently were back begging on the streets and blaming the government. It was enough to make any Conservative minister go 'beyond Wilding'.

Mr Luce's shake-up of the Arts Council was an attempt to break the mould of arts politics. The council had exercised its independence by allocating funds between its clients, forming its own judgment of the relative needs of major companies, like the Royal Opera House, and not-so-major companies like Gay Sweatshop. While any minister loses little sleep over the rise or demise of a Gay Sweatshop or two, a shut-down of the Royal Shakespeare Company in London is embarrassing. The government would obviously prefer money to be spent on famous companies whose complaints might give it a bad press. But the Arts Council always had the ready reply that on its meagre stipend it must support the nation's arts, great and small, and that government 'earmarking' of money, to favour companies the voters have heard of, would violate the famous arm's length principle.

Mr Luce's plan breaks up the Arts Council empire in which small companies have effectively sheltered behind big ones, and weakens the council's political leverage. The new council will have to concentrate on the Royal Opera House, while companies such as Gay Sweatshop take their chance with the regions. So, if the big companies struggle now, it may look more like council mismanagement and less like government meanness. Not many Arts Council chiefs would welcome that.

But Peter Palumbo did. He had been seen as government-friendly when he became chairman, and now the government had played the Palumbo card. As filing cabinets were moved out of the panelled boardrooms

Scene stealer or scene shifter?

Karl Phillips
Stage Technician

Photographed by
John Stoddart

ENGLISH NATIONAL OPERA — noted for the company we k
ENO 89/90 Season opens at the London Coliseum on August 24 1989

'But is it opera?' The English National Opera takes a bare-chested approach to marketing.

of 105 Piccadilly, once the Hotel Splendide and London *pied-à-terre* for a tsar, and into the new headquarters, the former premises of an Anglican missionary society in Victoria (conveniently shared with an office specialising in insolvency), the suspicion lingered in the minds of its substantially reduced staff that the council had been 'nobbled'.

Mr Palumbo had actually refurbished Piccadilly at his own expense, but his welcome for the move was genuine none the less, because it fitted his personal vision of national and regional 'centres of excellence'. It would enable the council to concentrate on the top companies, and, with less bureaucracy, allow time for more vision. This represents a return to an elitist interpretation of the council's role. Instead of launching a thousand little projects, it nurtures, in the words of a former secretary-general, 'few, but roses'.

Mr Palumbo also believes there is room for one extra 'rose'. A new unit, adding architecture and the preservation of cathedrals to the council's concerns, is under discussion. There has been an other-worldly tinge, too, to his earlier visions: of the nation's galleries and concert halls restored to a pristine state for the millennium; of a national 'City of Culture' for each year; and of a new era of arts patronage based on the generosity of fellow millionaires. Those concerned with more mundane matters, such as the lack of a national venue for dance, or the campaign for an arts lottery, find it harder to get his attention.

However, Mr Palumbo insists that none of this makes him a creature of the government. Indeed, he enjoys support in some unlikely quarters simply for his sincere love of art. His is a lofty, modernist, almost religious view of the arts, that of an aesthete, collector and connoisseur. In a speech defending the Arts Council reorganisation, he sounded a typically transcendent note: 'The artist is the most important individual in society, and, at its best, art is the highest expression of the human spirit.' Where government policy clashes with this 'aesthetic attitude' the chairman will not prove so compliant.

After the Ridley reshuffle, Mr Palumbo found another card-carrying arts-lover installed at the Office of Arts and Libraries in Horse Guards Road. David Mellor hoped it would count as a limited promotion: he would be running his own department, and paid for attending the opera. Anyone would be anxious to avoid being nicknamed 'the crab', after a series of sideways job moves, but the fact remained that the arts desk had not been a springboard to higher things in the past. As

Private Eye's 'Dear Bill' column put it: 'She doesn't consider ballet dancers worthy of discussion in the cabinet office.'

None the less, the minister's reputation as a rising star created high expectations in his new constituency. The Arts Council's new secretary-general, Anthony Everitt, immediately called for 'firm leadership in securing adequate funding'. Ominously, Mr Mellor learned that the outgoing minister had resisted a plea from Mrs Thatcher to stay on. Why had Mr Luce been so keen to leave? Apparently, because he felt he had no chance of repeating his *tour de force* at the treasury, and preferred to quit while he was ahead. Mr Luce's modest blood-from-a-stone act will in fact be hard to follow, yet Mr Mellor will be branded an immediate failure if he can't match it, and will only score points if he can better it. You can go off opera when you are forever being blamed for its decline.

Mr Mellor must also make a success of devolution, since the government is imposing it. This won't be much fun either. The political right urges him to make devolution his watchword, decentralising as many companies as possible, to break the power of the subsidised arts establishment, and reward market-oriented regional companies. Too much of this would alienate Mr Palumbo, who needs a 'respectable portfolio' of companies, to preserve the Arts Council's credibility. The government's guidelines on the matter, which say touring companies should stay, while those with an obvious base are devolved, were obviously going to be a battleground. Having just relinquished vice-chairmanship of the London Philharmonic Trust, David Mellor knows that its orchestra would always see itself as 'national', despite its 'local' name. But could the Arts Council justly keep one London orchestra, and not the other three? If all four, then what of the five outside? If all the big orchestras, then why not opera companies and theatres?

A scramble for big, established names was a natural consequence of the Arts Council's new, elitist-sounding emphasis on 'excellence', and, by implication, first- and second-class companies. The more subtle 'Rittner interpretation' of its role would have emphasised support for innovative companies, which, though smaller, actually need more nurturing. Dozens of famous examples were dreading a takeover by the weakest regional bureaucracy, London, in what one director compared to a local clay pigeon shoot taking over NATO. The region's optimistically-named Andrew Brill has tried to be reassuring about its 'loony

'In spite of the film's clearly abusive content, I do not wish to seek the dubious protection of censorship . . . Publication is the surest way of revealing its shabbiness and of preventing it from becoming a *cause célèbre.'*
Salman Rushdie on the banning of the film International Guerillas

left' reputation ('We don't expect dance companies to employ one-legged ballerinas. We are not Stalinists') but, after protests, his board is to be completely replaced. Expert advisers will be urgently needed there, as in Birmingham, or Bournemouth, which must assess the needs of their famous orchestras, without the benefit of comparable cases. Judging from the difficulty the Arts Council has filling its panels, there may not be enough experts to go round.

After struggling to make other people's visions work, Mr Mellor may feel his best chance of making an impact lies in having some of his own, and influencing the national arts strategy, a policy manifesto which has to be ready by 1992. He could start with a clearer definition of the complementary roles of private sponsorship and public subsidy. His predecessor's policy contribution was to push sponsorship, by offering bonus grants for companies which found sponsors. Those very companies then found themselves in deep trouble as sponsorship proved no substitute for guaranteed income. The sponsors, who want to be associated with glitter and success, not threatened closures, feel used, and need to be won over.

If the government had hoped sponsors would tame the arts, it now finds them among its sharpest critics, and none more so than the biggest sponsor, Royal Insurance, in the person of its chief executive, Ian Rushton. After making headlines with a record £2 million for the Royal Shakespeare Company, he gained extra publicity by lambasting the government for not clearing the national companies' deficits. With their promise of plentiful jam (provided their logo is writ large on it), the sponsors are putting pressure on the government to guarantee bread and butter.

The RSC has long been a Conservative *bête noire*, but Mr Mellor would be wise to look carefully at its case. Not only has it won record sponsorship, but it earns £1 million a year from the commercial success of *Les Misérables*. It actually pays more back in tax than it takes in subsidy, and under Labour's VAT concessions would be in profit. Its champions say it gives more pleasure than any other theatre company in the world, reaching a million people a year. The imminent end of Terry Hands's difficult reign as artistic director might provide a convenient moment for a reconciliation, if Mr Mellor were looking for one.

The mood of government arts policy, wanting to join the party but hesitating over the ticket price, was summed up in June. 'Leading lights of the film world', both of them in fact, were invited to Number Ten for a movie summit. When 'leading lights of the television world' had been similarly invited it had ended in a row about the unions. But Sir Richard Attenborough and David Puttnam found a new atmosphere and even some cash; £5 million towards European co-productions, and £150,000 towards a worthy Euro-film award. Better than nothing (our previous contribution), but well short of a Damascus Road conversion. Mrs Thatcher, her new enthusiasm for film perhaps stimulated by having watched *Gandhi* and *Cry Freedom* on video, asked: 'Why didn't you come and see me ten years ago?' Sir Richard apparently replied: 'Because you didn't invite me . . . darling.'

While cultural policy remains on hold, paintings and other western art treasures are disappearing to Japan at a rate of a million a year. The art market, symbolising the triumph of commercialism, is best served if anything at all can be a potential 'masterpiece', irrespective of its aesthetic worth. As art has increased in value more than any other asset this century, the public's reaction to paintings has been distorted, galleries have been priced out of the market and idealistic young artists have become disillusioned with conventional painting.

However, the distortion is largely because of one eccentric factor, Japan, and in 1990 this cynical roller-coaster was actually checked a little. Auction records were smashed again by Renoir, and then Van Gogh, whose 'Portrait of Dr Gachet', at £50 million, contributed to a Sotheby's record of £175 million-worth of business in a single sale. But this was because one Japanese collector, Ryeoi Sato, regarded the paintings as 'quite cheap, and very reasonable'. The underlying trend showed a sharp drop in demand for mediocre work, and the market is at last showing more aesthetic discrimination.

The ever-increasing difficulty of stemming the flow of works abroad was underlined by the saga of 'The Three Graces', a neo-classical masterpiece by the nineteenth-century Italian sculptor Antonio Canova, commissioned by the Fourth Duke of Bedford and housed in a specially-built temple at Woburn Abbey. The British Council had exhibited it in Washington as an example of the treasures of our stately homes, only to discover that it wasn't; it had already been sold for £1.2 million, via a shadowy Cayman Islands company. When the mystery buyer then applied to export it to the United States for £7.6 million, the exhibition organisers concluded that their show had been exploited to advertise the piece and boost the price.

Anish Kapoor, named 'most promising young artist' at the Venice Biennale.

While the export was temporarily suspended, the Victoria and Albert Museum had to launch an appeal without being able to tell supporters who their money was going to. Concerned peers besieged the government; Lord St John of Fawsley, a former arts minister, called for an end to the secrecy which hampered such appeals, and Lord Rothschild offered to buy the sculpture for the nation in lieu of tax. But the government's only concession was one more likely to be welcomed by businessmen with big cheque-books; in future they, as well as museums, would be allowed to buy works destined for export.

Faced with what to them is simply an additional threat, heritage groups are resorting to the courts, in a last effort to influence the government. In the case of 'The Three Graces', this involves a legal challenge to the department of the environment for ever letting the sculpture out of its temple, which is a listed building. Conservationists have proved this tactic can work by winning a completely different case, concerning a government decision allowing the demolition of eight listed buildings in the City. The environment secretary had been persuaded that a replacement buiding, proposed by Peter Palumbo, 'just might be a masterpiece'. But the high court ruled that even a minister capable of such aesthetic judgments was subject to planning law. The judge may have been swayed by the Prince of Wales's comparison of the new design to a '1930s wireless', particularly as this had been delivered in the manner of a 1930s broadcaster.

In pop music, an art form more likely to be patronised by the Princess of Wales, landmarks cannot be protected from the advance of commerce. Before the British Phonographic Industry's traditional 'chart' was itself 'busted', in July, in favour of a cheaper newcomer, it recorded a chilling statistic. Stock, Aitken and Waterman, the Minogue/Donovan people, overtook the Lennon/McCartney record of having a song in the top forty for three and a half years. Jason (teenage girl fainting ratio – five per minute) has sold 10 million records in a year. Kylie (her name means boomerang – but she hasn't yet) has made Britain's best-selling debut album. It's little comfort that the Stock, Aitken and Waterman hit factory, which boasts it can produce four songs a day may soon have been seen off by an American manufacturer. New Kids Off The Production Line (sorry – On The Block) learnt to mime at thirteen and come complete with a cartoon series and matching wallpaper.

'Authentic' (forty-something) rockers haven't escaped the marketing men either. They do mega-tours, 1990 being a mega-year: Clapton (eighteen-night marathon at the Albert Hall); Bowie (book-a-song-in-advance-service); Stones (twenty-month Evian-water-backstage-please world tour). These can now be enjoyed in mega-comfort. One credit card call secures a return flight to Paris, two nights in a smart hotel and a guaranteed mega-seat for Phil Collins. Given that pop is one of Britain's most vital art forms, there are worry-ingly few signs of rebellion. But dance music in the acid-house/hip-hop/rap vein has created its own route to the charts, via the clubs. And 'indy bands' (independent of big labels, with left-of-centre views and anoraks) have got into the charts on the strength of a hard-earned regional following. The Manchester band, Stone Roses, reached the top ten without appearing on television. Now that a studio track can be recorded for as little as £250 the pop geniuses of tomorrow at least have a fighting chance.

Daniel Day-Lewis as Christy Brown in *My Left Foot,* winner of the 'Best Actor' award in the 1990 Oscars.

According to one influential art critic, Peter Fuller, who died in April, the future of the arts in Britain will be shaped by a struggle between the aesthetes and the philistines. In his view, 'philistines of the left', who dismiss beautiful paintings as a branch of capitalism, and encourage artists to undertake political 'projects', have formed an unholy alliance with 'philistines of the right', who treat art works as 'products', and the arts as a leisure industry, advertising the Victoria and Albert Museum, as 'an ace caff with quite a nice museum attached'. Both oppose the 'aesthetic view of life' – the search for lasting spiritual values in art.

If so, the aesthetes may be rallying their forces. When several senior curators from the Victoria and Albert were ousted in a shake-up aimed at making the museum more accessible, they formed a Save the V&A campaign, and harassed the new regime with pamphlets alleging that scholarship had been cheapened. The

1990 FILM OSCARS

BEST...
PICTURE: *Driving Miss Daisy.*
ACTOR: Daniel Day-Lewis, *My Left Foot.*
ACTRESS: Jessica Tandy, *Driving Miss Daisy.*
DIRECTOR: Oliver Stone, *Born on the Fourth of July.*
ORIGINAL SCREENPLAY: Tom Schulman, *Dead Poets Society.*
FOREIGN FILM: *Cinema Paradiso* (Italy).

new director, Elizabeth Esteve-Coll, acknowledged that she was up against the 'Courtauld mafia', graduates of the Courtauld Institute in key museum posts, who are seen by the new brooms of the museum world as secretive hoarders of their connoisseur knowledge, and who fail to communicate with the public. As if rising to the challenge, the Courtauld this year opened its own private collection to the public.

As the struggle ensues, the aesthetic camp can claim some friends in high places. Peter Palumbo, himself a connoisseur, is with them in emphasising the creative genius of the individual artist. Symbolically, he had erected in the council's entrance an abstract by the sculptor by Anthony Caro, who once summed up the sovereignty of the artist by saying, 'sculpture can be anything'. But perhaps closer to Peter Fuller's philosophy is the Prince of Wales, who, with his 'ten commandments for architecture', also believes the artist must respect absolute values derived from nature and tradition. At the prince's new summer school in Oxford, students begin by religiously copying the five classical orders of Roman and Renaissance architecture. Palumbo and the prince both take an aesthetic view of architecture, but clashed head on over what should be built. Their disagreement contains the seeds of a larger debate for the Nineties, about the true nature of aesthetic values.

'When you are lying drunk at the airport, you're Irish. When you win an Oscar, you're British.'
Brenda Fricker, who won the Oscar for 'Best Supporting Actress' for My Left Foot

MEDIA REVOLUTION

Did more media in 1990 mean better?

As people were offered a bewildering variety of

new newspapers and radio and television

channels, the Calcutt report, the broadcasting

bill and the recession sounded warning notes

Peter Fiddick

O n the face of it, this was the year in which an exciting new range of choices was unfolded before the viewers, listeners and readers of Britain. On offer were new national newspapers, many new local radio stations and one new national network, and a clutch of new television channels with the promise of more to come. Compared with the cautious, controlled way most of the British media, public and private enterprise alike, have evolved through the past four decades, here was a veritable explosion of new sounds, new voices, new ideas. Just consider the main elements of it all.

In the spring, BSB (British Satellite Broadcasting), the long-awaited, much-delayed provider of new television channels via a high-power satellite beaming straight to small dishes in our homes, got on the air. So five services on four channels were added to the terrestrial quartet (BBC1 and BBC2, ITV, Channel 4) and the cluster of new satellite channels, including Sky, which had become available to British audiences via a Luxemburg-based satellite company just a year earlier. By the end of the year, Sky and the SES-Astra company alone were dangling sixteen channels before potential subscribers, with the promise of another sixteen to come from the second Astra satellite planned for 1991.

And while the new direct-to-home (DTH) satellite television systems were either grabbing headlines or buying acres of advertising space to lay out their rival packages of movies, sport, news, rock and the rest, the alternative way of distributing television channels by the dozen was stirring. After a decade of fitful growth, barely one million British homes (out of 20 million) were even within reach of such a system, and fewer than 200,000 had actually opted to be connected. By mid-summer, when the cable authority closed its books, licences to lay new cable systems had been distributed to dozens of companies whose franchise areas would bring the cable option within reach of three-quarters of the population within a few years.

Radio, too, was moving into a new era. Nearly two decades after local radio – BBC and ILR – was officially started, the pirates were given a chance to come in from the cold, trading the buccaneering world of playing what they liked, in the way they liked, at the cost of sporadic raids from the department of trade and industry's growing band of spoil-sports, for the opportunity to aim at audiences the established stations had not thought of – and getting the advertising revenue their illicit activities had denied them.

So, around the turn of the year, a couple of dozen new stations were given the green light – not all of them reformed pirates, to be sure, but all given their licences on the strength of a promise to reach different sorts of audiences: here the jazz fans, there the ethnic groups, even, in one case, those radicals reckoned to want middle-of-the-road music without the meanderings of the DJ: 'Radio without the speakers' was Melody Radio's pitch to the London region. Elsewhere in the spectrum, other user-friendly new names like Jazz FM, Buzz FM, Sunset, even, indeed, Spectrum, set themselves before the

BSB's Chief Executive, Anthony Simonds-Gooding, and his deputy, John Gau, toast the channel's launch.

135

public. This was not the full radio revolution – that, as outlined in government policy, will facilitate some hundreds of small stations and a trio of advertising-financed national networks – but it was the start. The scattering of new-style stations would bring fresh competition to places where commercial radio was already established and be the pathfinders for the glories to come.

Then there was print. Britain's national newspapers had undergone their own revolution earlier in the Eighties, when Rupert Murdoch's crushing of trades union power in the four titles he then owned

A new Sunday newspaper for the A's and B's, and a weekly with an eye to 1992. Meanwhile, in September the *Sunday Correspondent* was forced to relaunch in tabloid form.

opened the way for other proprietors to do the new deals on manning and technology that promised a long-sought profitability. It seemed also to open the way for new publishers to enter the market, though the first effort, Eddie Shah's *Today*, had in the event done no more than bounce into the hands of one established proprietor and out again into those of Mr Murdoch himself. But a new quality daily newspaper, *The Independent*, had been born and successfully established, and during 1989 plans had been unveiled for a new quality Sunday paper, the *Sunday Correspondent*, which might similarly offer an alternative to those who felt there might be intelligent life beyond *The Observer*, *The Sunday*

Telegraph and whatever nucleus of thought might be found within the multiplying sections of *The Sunday Times*.

At which point, the new boy swiftly joined the club. *The Independent*, acting like any Fleet Street proprietor of yore, in the spring of 1989 announced its own Sunday sister-paper, an overt pre-emptive strike against the threatened interloper, aimed at depriving it of backers. The *Sunday Correspondent* was nevertheless launched in September 1989, and, in February 1990, *The Independent on Sunday* arrived, a fifth title bidding for the attention of serious-minded people on a Sunday, where months earlier there had been three (and a quarter-century before that, in the trendy Sixties, only two). More was on its way. Come the summer, Robert Maxwell, ebullient proprietor of the Mirror group of newspapers, actually achieved what he had been promising for two years and more, and launched *The European*, a weekly newspaper with the lofty and timely ideal of speaking with one voice (and for the moment one language, English) to readers throughout the Continent, in recognition of the new European system shortly to come.

A year, then, of expansion, competition, confidence, and the heady idealism, the freeing of ideas and creativity, that all this can engender? Well, not exactly.

For many in the media, and many in their audiences, 1990 was the year of the hard grind, of a game played on an uneven pitch and with ever-changing rules. There were indeed those for whom, by the year's end, the game they started out playing seemed to have been part-way won, but, by the same year's end, the goalposts were on the move.

Look back at those earlier examples from a different perspective. The DTH satellite television revolution? True, by the end of the year the British viewers' take-up of the new deal – about £300 for the necessary dish and decoder, plus a monthly subscription fee for such prime attractions as the feature film channels, whether from Sky or BSB – was building. It seemed possible that there might be more than one million homes with their own satellite receiving dishes by Christmas. Even so, as the key autumn season began, analysts were still divided as to when either would be operating at a profit – perhaps two more years for Sky, four for BSB was one estimate – or whether there could ever be room for both. The disadvantages of having rival systems, each demanding its own receiving equipment, neither capable of relaying the other, were evident in the tens of millions of pounds expended in advertising and

'**The Independent** had put its tanks on our lawn . . . quite deliberately it decided to occupy **The Times's** territory. I have no doubt in my mind that we have to try to reoccupy it. **The Independent** is our prime target.'
Simon Jenkins, who succeeded Charles Wilson as editor of The Times

Sky's the limit –
satellite
television
comes to a
council estate in
South London.

direct-marketing material. It was suspected that many people, whatever they told opinion pollsters, were continuing to sit tight and wait to see which side won.

Such a position is the perfect opportunity for cable television, which can save the individual viewer the trouble of having multiple receiving devices, of whatever sort, and simply collect all the signals and pump them down the high-tech, fibre-optic, interactive cable. However, the flurry of activity in the cable business in Britain in 1990 was not yet greatly to do with selling subscriptions. More it was the outcome of a ruling that would-be cable system operators who didn't get their applications in very quickly, and undertake to start constructing their network soon, would find rather tougher conditions applying to future franchisees. If the sudden rush could not properly be seen as the result of coercion, it could reasonably be said to be stemming from a more blatant use of the stick-and-carrot school of management than the media are normally inclined to accept. And, to the extent that many of us should shortly begin to get the letters on our doormat, seducing us to sign up, it might well have worked.

The questions, however, remain. How many will sign up? And for how long? And which programmes will turn out to be the main attractions? The considerable risks in the cable television business may be indicated by the extent to which many of the new franchise holders are backed by American or even French money, rather than British.

Even the newspaper developments had an American financial connection. The *Sunday Correspondent* launched and received a decently respectful reception from its peers (though mostly not, of course, in their own pages). But it did not achieve its target circulation, thought to be some 350,000–400,000 a week, roughly half the sales of the longer-established *Observer* and *Sunday Telegraph*. Neither, for that matter, did the new *Independent on Sunday*, despite the existence of the daily *Independent* as a promotional instrument. By midsummer, *The Sunday Times* was boasting that it had the circulation of *The Observer* and *The Sunday Telegraph* put together, while they could at least say that the two new papers combined still didn't match either of their circulations. As the *Sunday Correspondent*'s sales slipped back to 200,000 and under, its backers had to make tough decisions, whereupon it emerged that the single most important backer, a Chicago-based newspaper group, was perfectly prepared to switch horses and back *The Independent* instead. The Americans' price proved too high for *The Independent*'s view of its independence, and the *Sunday Correspondent*'s other shareholders (which by now included *The Independent*'s daily rival, *The Guardian*) also resisted.

The upshot was curiously reminiscent of the early days of that first harbinger of 'the Fleet Street revolution', *Today*. This time, however, it was not Murdoch, but the rival press tycoon, Robert Maxwell, who emerged from the shadows to take a stake in the *Sunday Correspondent*, and to take over its printing contract, with a change of editor and a change of format as part of the deal. At the end of September, the *Sunday Correspondent* re-launched as a tabloid.

But this is not the story of one new newspaper's birth-pangs. The uncomfortable fact was that the *Sunday Correspondent*'s arrival served only to emphasise the problems the national newspapers had to confront in 1990. It was the year in which, at best, growth stopped. Even *The Sunday Times*, poised to have such a commanding lead in the quality Sunday market that all rivals would be squeezed, found that new sales and advertising revenue were not easy to come by. Its older rivals, trimmed by new competitors not able to reach their targets, were forced into job-saving economies. Even Rupert Murdoch's main cash-cow, the down-market *Sun*, was contributing proportionately less to the multi-million pound funding of his hungry satellite television venture. And, throughout the year, rumours continued that Conrad Black, the Canadian owner of the Telegraph group, was moving in on United Newspapers, whose Express newspapers offered another three national titles.

And then there was radio. At the end of August, the BBC launched its new network, Radio 5. It has to be said that the expectations of many professional observers (inside the corporation and out) were not high; and that the initial reaction to the new service confounded those sceptical expectations. Radio 5 had been devised in the face of government insistance that broadcasters should not occupy two frequencies with the same service. In putting Radios 1, 2, 3 and 4 on to single FM frequencies (though also keeping Radio 4 on long wave), the BBC was left with schools, sports and some other broadcasts, which it then used as the core of the new Radio 5, adding new programmes for children, some World Service relays and other elements. The problem, for the current orthodoxy about people's use of broadcasting, was that here was a service offering different things to different people at different times: 'targeting' carefully defined audiences is the modern way. But Radio 5 went on air at the end of August to cautiously enthusiastic professional comment followed by audience research indicating that, despite the disruption to Radio 2, whose AM frequencies it took, total audiences had indeed gone up.

Meanwhile, the feedback from the new commercial stations was less promising. These were to be 'targeted', if anything ever was. The rationale behind them was that, pending the government's legislation setting up a new radio authority to oversee a wide-scale expansion, these new 'incremental' stations should be allowed to bid for particular audiences in areas where there were already well-established independent local radio stations. Hence, a range of programme plans, from the London jazz station to others seeking particular ethnic groups. Whatever the professional principles, the results were disappointing. Even a station which drew favourable comment for its programming like Jazz FM was evidently going to face difficulties in building the advertising revenue by which alone it must live. Others, very quickly, were under critical financial pressure which in turn quickly forced changes both in management and in programme plans.

The uncomfortable truth had been dawning on some since early in the year. The British economy was in trouble. And however much, in the early months, government and such circles disclaimed talk about a full-scale recession being at hand, the media felt the chill early. It is a familiar pattern: industry and commerce sense sales and profits dropping, look for economies, and trim advertising budgets.

First to feel the effect are the new media – satellite television, commercial radio – which have not yet won advertising agencies' confidence. Then the print media are squeezed, depending on their specialist audiences. By this time, too, the advertising industry itself is feeling the pain. It happened in 1990. Jobs were shed. At least one high-profile London agency, Yellowhammer, went under. And the outfit with the highest profile of all, Saatchi and Saatchi, one of the most aggressive players in the global expansion game of the 1980s, was forced to make top management changes as both profits and share-price went on the slide.

Commercial television, normally, is the last to feel the draught, and the most cushioned. Such is the perceived power of television that advertisers who feel they have a choice tend to cut other advertising expenditure first. Nevertheless, by August 1990, Britain's ITV companies were reporting monthly advertising revenue down by 20 per cent, year on year, and prospects of a major reversal of the trend were slim.

But for television the main story of 1990 was a problem of a different kind. It was the year in which the long argument over the Conservative government's view of the shape of television in the future came to a head. Most of the second half of the decade had been occupied by the debate. At its heart was the proposal that, in future, licences to broadcast in the ITV system should be awarded to the companies that made the government the highest cash bid for them. Around this many other proposals were structured, all aimed at bringing market forces to bear on what the government and its advisers saw as a 'cosy duopoly' in which the publicly-funded BBC formed one arm, the ITV network, with its closely-linked sibling Channel 4, the other. Now, regulations were to be loosened, demands that commercial television operate under public service constraints relaxed, and commercial efficiency was to be the key to success. The debate had lasted more than two years, during which ITV led the argument that the 'auction' of contracts, in particular, would make the entire network vulnerable to takeover by big-money gamblers who would put profits before programmes; 1990 brought the crucial stage, in which the government brought its broadcasting bill to parliament.

It seems now as though a political accident crucially affected the outcome. Late in 1989, the chancellor of the exchequer, Nigel Lawson, resigned. The ensuing reshuffle brought in a new home secretary and, below him, a new minister of state for the broadcasting portfolio. It was David Mellor who would guide the broadcasting bill through the House of Commons. To general astonishment, he both agreed and delivered significant changes, softening the full market-force thrust of the bill, accepting the replacement of some of the former public service requirements, and conceding to the proposed new Independent Television Commission (ITC), successor to the Independent Broadcasting Authority, some discretion in judging the quality and realism of an applicant's programme plans rather than having automatically to accept the highest bid.

For both the existing ITV companies and outsiders interested in bidding for a place in the new era of the main commercial channel, beginning in 1993, these were major victories. On this basis, the new broadcasting act might not be perfect, but it would be workable. The sense of relief increased in September, when the chairman-designate of the ITC, George Russell, announced that the division of the ITV system into fifteen geographical regions would not be changed for the next set of contracts, thereby assuring even the smallest and most vulnerable regional companies that there would at least still be contracts to bid for.

Even so, it was clear that the new world was going to be very different – and for Channel 4, too, which will sell its own advertising airtime and no longer be linked so closely with ITV. The preparations for the coming challenge were painful in themselves, with the need to reduce costs, and the effects of another government demand – that more programmes should be commissioned from independent production companies – causing ITV and BBC alike to create new, slimmer structures and, in particular, to cut back sharply on the

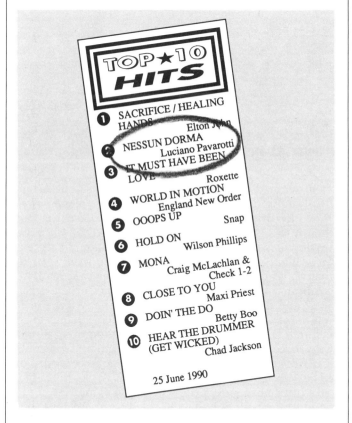

TOP ★ 10 HITS

❶ SACRIFICE / HEALING HANDS
Elton John

❷ NESSUN DORMA
Luciano Pavarotti

❸ IT MUST HAVE BEEN LOVE
Roxette

❹ WORLD IN MOTION
England New Order

❺ OOOPS UP
Snap

❻ HOLD ON
Wilson Phillips

❼ MONA
Craig McLachlan & Check 1-2

❽ CLOSE TO YOU
Maxi Priest

❾ DOIN' THE DO
Betty Boo

❿ HEAR THE DRUMMER (GET WICKED)
Chad Jackson

25 June 1990

Pavarotti and Puccini hit the pop charts with World Cup theme tune 'Nessun Dorma', from the opera _Turandot_.

number of people on the staff payroll.

I am well aware that this survey has concentrated almost totally on the media's structural and economic issues. Here we are, considering the role of the biggest providers of entertainment and information in our society, and there is no mention of programmes, or scoops, or ideas. It is not, of course, that there were no high points, or lows. It might be tempting to say that

**Neighbours –
1,000
programmes
and still going
strong.**

1990 seemed to be the year when cartoon characters finally took over. The cult of the *Teenage Mutant Hero Turtles* hit Britain, followed shortly by *The Simpsons*. But then it was also the year when Peter Greenaway's TV version of Dante's *Inferno* reached the Channel 4 screen, as brilliant a piece of innovation as we have seen in many a year. As the influence of soap opera spread, we celebrated both the thirtieth anniversary of *Coronation Street* and the one-thousandth edition of *Neighbours*. It was the year, on the other hand, in which – thanks to an inspired choice in the BBC's presentation of its World Cup soccer coverage – Luciano Pavarotti and Puccini's aria *Nessun Dorma* hit the pop charts at the expense of Kylie Minogue and Jason Donovan.

Journalism, too, produced much of interest, some good, some bad. For all its problems, the *Sunday Correspondent*, in its original form, struck not a few of us as a welcome addition to Sundays. We were treated to the riotous spectacle of two other Sunday newspaper editors, Andrew Neil of *The Sunday Times* and Peregrine Worsthorne, former editor of *The Sunday Telegraph*, playing out in contrasting styles a courtroom drama over the latter's view of the former's private life. A less edifying spat came when an *Observer* journalist, Farzad Bazoft, was executed in Iraq for alleged espionage, and

Sunday Times Editor, Andrew Neil, in buoyant mood after the Pamella Bordes libel trial.

'If *The Sunday Times* had won more than derisory damages, it would have been a victory for censorship. As it is, it is a victory for free speech.'
Peregrine Worsthorne, former editor of The Sunday Telegraph, *who criticised Andrew Neil for his relationship with Pamella Bordes*

'It is a victory for the new Britain against the old Britain.'
Andrew Neil, editor of The Sunday Times, *after being awarded £1,000 damages*

some other newspapers were quick to accept stories apparently designed to discredit the dead man.

But that, of course, was but a foretaste of things to come, when Iraq's invasion of Kuwait in August gave print and electronic journalists alike a challenge of technique and of philosophy that would test them most severely. The first and most obvious development was the role of the new twenty-four-hour television news operators, notably America's CNN, who became part of the conduct of the confrontation, as the political leaders on both sides sought to use television to put pressure on each other.

Observer journalist Farzad Bazoft, executed for alleged spying by Iraq earlier this year.

Nevertheless, even in these areas, the outstanding issues of this year were the structural ones, of economics and of politics. The broadcasting bill, bearing mainly on ITV and Channel 4, was the biggest, but there were others. The press found itself under pressure from government to put its house in order in its treatment of the privacy of individuals, when the report of a committee under David Calcutt QC recommended the abolition of the Press Council, the establishment of a new self-regulatory body with teeth, the creation of new criminal offences of invasion of privacy – and the threat of tougher, statutory means if self-monitoring was perceived not to work. And from another front came a move, spearheaded in the House of Lords, to inject into the broadcasting bill new rules designed to limit further the expression of personal views in television and radio programmes.

It is issues such as these, together with the effects of economic pressures, that are always playing a major role in the way our media operate, and what they deliver. Often, they are working unseen. In 1990, they were out in the open, subjects of crucial debate and decision. But it was a year of troubled transition, whose outcome is still unknown.

The SPORTING YEAR

The cricket tourists in South Africa

found politics embedded in their

sport, while the World Cup in Italy

had Gazza – and all of England's

fans – in tears

Archie Macpherson

As sport entered the new decade it was clear that no major sporting event could expect to be immune from outside pressures of one kind or another. A number of major sporting events took place in 1990 but they managed to withstand external pressures and became memorable in the end chiefly for the sport itself.

The Commonwealth Games – so riven by political dispute in the past – was being given its last chance for survival, for example. Multiracial cricket looked on the verge of disintegration. Domestic football seemed as if it might atrophy under the imposition of an identity-card scheme. The World Cup in Italy appeared to be the perfect scene for the enactment of a footballing Armageddon. And international athletics looked as if it could disappear underneath the sleaze of drug scandals. This unhealthy agenda for confrontation and conflict was curiously enough largely set in the first month of the year and anxious eyes were turned in particular to London on 24 January when, by one of these coincidences which might have been deviously arranged by some *agent provocateur*, two cricket parties set out in opposite directions. According to the opponents of the rebel tour, the two groups would be morally as well as geographically thousands of miles apart.

The English cricketers heading for their 'rebel' South African tour created more fuss and drew more attention than the official party flying to the West Indies. After all the official England team was merely heading for that boring old English ritual of being demolished by West Indian fast bowling. They were simply going to play cricket.

The others, heading for the southern hemisphere, were aggravating – unwittingly or otherwise – political sensitivities. In New Zealand's Commonwealth Games circles – where the name South Africa is rarely mentioned and only with a sharp intake of breath – they had heard that the Johannesburg police had used batons and tear gas on a crowd which was waiting to demonstrate peacefully on the arrival of the sixteen cricketers at the airport. They could not have imagined anything worse happening so near the opening of the Games short of an incendiary device being thrown into the newly completed Mount Smart Stadium.

But they did not need to hold their nerve too long. Within a few days, the caucus of African nations decided that the response to the tour would not be a boycott but a demand for some form of censure to be delivered during the congress of the Commonwealth Games Federation. Although anything was possible in the volatile situation, most of us out there were none too surprised by that decision. The Africans did not wish to embarrass their hosts who had a highly credible record in the stand against apartheid. It was also felt they could no longer disadvantage their own athletes by playing the now rather hackneyed Commonwealth Games boycott card. The Africans further believed that black South Africans would mount a sufficiently effective protest without any aid from the other side of the world.

They were right in that. The tour became something of a moveable siege. The attempts by the players, especially the leading lights like Gatting and Graveney, at imperturbability (largely induced by their two-year contract said to be worth £80,000) began to resemble insensitive intransigence. Affecting an innocent air about the consequences of apartheid seemed quite the wrong posture to adopt, especially when supplemented by remarks like Gatting's after three days of the initial demonstrations which he described as 'a lot of singing and dancing'.

From the outset, the demonstrations were bigger, more organised and more clamorous than they had bargained for. Of the demonstrations held at Kimberley for the first match of the tour Ali Bacher admitted, when the tour had been eventually cut short, 'I was frightened. I never told the players, but it was much worse than I feared. There was a great deal of anxiety.'

As the scoreboard at the Wanderers cricket ground at the first test revealed the humbling of the tourists heading for defeat against the South African national side, a black protester outside the ground held up another scorecard: 'English XI: 180; black South Africans retired hurt due to you (buckshot 25, tear gas 60, clubs 42, dogs 12)'.

The intertwining of sport and politics culminating in violence against demonstrators was the last thing President F. W. de Klerk wanted beamed round the world as he himself headed into uncharted waters with the ANC and the release of Nelson Mandela which occurred halfway through the tour. His placid countenance and his dignified utterances contrasted effectively with the turmoil surrounding the cricket. Supplemented by the unbanning of the ANC it seemed that historic events were consolidating views along the political spectrum that the cricketers' visit was a quite unnecessary aggravation that would be better put out of the way.

Behind the scenes the ANC put pressure on its own National Sports Congress (NSC) to reach a deal with the South African Cricket Union (SACU) to abort the tour. They compromised and, with an NSC guarantee that there would be no more demonstrations, SACU agreed to abandon the second five-day international and limit the rest of the itinerary to four limited-overs matches.

One month after they had set out from England the cricketers returned to London as the cost of the tour was assessed. The uneventful cricket which had been played had been quickly forgotten. The original intention of Ali Bacher to increase involvement of the players in the black townships had failed so badly it seemed as if it had all along been a gross miscalculation on his part. Indeed, the view of the opponents of the tour was that the cause of non-racial cricket had been badly damaged. Out of this wreckage the cricketers brought back considerable booty which was why they had been willing to take on the wrath of the anti-apartheid forces in the first place. Although Mike Gatting admitted only to receiving 40 per cent of the original contract, that still amounted to a large sum of money.

Those younger players like Jarvis, Wells and Maynard who might have worried about their uncertain futures would have taken some comfort out of the ironic situation in the West Indies where a man who

England's man for all seasons. Graham Gooch's batting dominated in the West Indies in the winter and in England in the summer.

once was regarded as something of a pariah in the Caribbean was leading England in a tour which was making us revise our ideas of their ingrained inferiority. The official tourists were doing famously under the captaincy of Graham Gooch. Gooch was a veteran of several South African campaigns. He had wintered there in the sun, drew opprobrium from the usual quarters, was dropped from the official scene and yet had survived to become legit again. Given that the normal odds against them to perform well against the West Indies were increased by the emasculating defection of the rebels, it seemed that the world had been turned upside down when on 24 February, the day the rebels left South Africa, the loyalists dismissed the home side in the first test at Kingston, Jamaica, for 164.

This was more stunning than the news that bitter demonstrations had been held in South Africa because it was least expected. Angus Fraser's five for 28 seemed hardly credible and Allan Lamb's 132 the following day bordered on the miraculous for English batting against the West Indies had, for over a decade, had the staying power of a soap bubble. At that moment those achievements might have been regarded as freakish and perhaps not worthy of serious interpretation. But even after an entire fourth day lost through rain, something of a more elemental nature seemed to be stirring when Devon Malcolm, a native son of Jamaica, took Viv Richards's wicket for the second time in the game and in achieving four for 77 in the second innings helped England to their first test match victory over the West Indies in sixteen years. Cricket writers refurbished their superlatives and the enjoyment of victory seemed an act of liberation.

But no amount of preparedness could foil the rain. A personalised cloud seemed to follow the side from island to island. It rained on every stop. The second test was abandoned without a ball being bowled. But, more cruelly, in Port of Spain in the third test the game was called off because of atrocious light with England only 31 runs away from their second win and five wickets in hand. Even more significant was that they lost their leader Graham Gooch whose finger was broken by an Ezra Mosely delivery. In the context of the excellent preparation and the disciplined approach to the challenge which he set by personal example this was a bitter blow. He was to take no further part in the remaining two tests.

'I know I look like a totally miserable sod on television. I wish I didn't but there you are.'
Graham Gooch, England cricket captain

The West Indies assumption of superiority had been severely dented however, and there were distinct signs of wear and tear. In Port of Spain they sent down only 17 overs in 100 minutes and looked like men seeking divine intervention. In the final test Viv Richards took the trouble to climb into the press-box even as his team took to the field to berate a journalist for an article he had written for a paper in England. The scribes regard such behaviour on their hallowed territory as slanging the vicar at prayer. They duly demolished Viv in the copy they sent home to their editors.

Yet the West Indies won the final two tests to win the series 2–1. England might justifiably have claimed that had the clouds not thickened as if to the entreaty of a rain dance, and had Graham Gooch's finger been made of cast iron, then the outcome would have been different. But defeat was less important than the reassertion of pride and the timely surfacing of latent abilities which were exhibited both by the veterans and the novices. Both categories had merged to give English cricket a backbone that few had thought existed before the tour had started. After all, under Mickey Stewart's stewardship they had lost four out of five series without a single test victory. A debacle coming on top of the defection of the rebels might have dealt a death blow to the English game. Instead, the official tourists' performance, against all the odds, made the South African tour seem even more squalid. By comparison with those who had chased the Rand, the official tourists appeared almost noble.

This made the English cricketing summer all the sweeter. It was appropriately dominated by Gooch who coped well with the New Zealanders and almost single-handedly suffocated the Indians. His massive 333 at Lord's looked like a man taking permanent root in his own acre and, although the Indians batted beautifully, Gooch's 1,058 test runs in a single summer had put him above the record of 974 previously set by Don Bradman. For a man who had once been considered beyond the pale because of his South African connections, joining the pantheon of the greats meant his restitution was well and truly complete.

The Commonwealth Games in Auckland had survived largely intact. More than fifty Commonwealth states had taken part compared with Edinburgh's twenty-eight. The financial scandal which had affected the organising committee's chairman David Johnstone and caused his resignation only sixty days before the opening had been coped with well by those who remained to look after affairs. The New Zealand government gave an undertaking to underwrite the Games to the extent of NZ$20 million and, in the end, because of the realisation of certain sponsorships and a late surge of ticket sales, their ultimate grant fell well within the limit. But the vital principle seemed to have been re-established within the Commonwealth movement that if the Games were to continue into the future they would require public funding. Certainly the future hosts of Victoria 1994 were immediately guaranteed Canadian federal support. The British government now seemed quite isolated in its view that major events like the Commonwealth Games ought to be wholly self-financing.

But Auckland was not entirely untainted. Two Welsh weightlifters, Ricky Chaplin and Garry Hives, were disqualified and given life bans for having tested positive for drug-taking. Along with an Indian, Paul Subratakumar, they left New Zealand in ignominy and reminded us that the Ben Johnson legacy had to be thorough vigilance.

Political scrutiny of the sporting arena had never been as intense as through the proposed football spectators bill. After the disaster at the Heysel Stadium in Brussels, the prime minister had become closely associated with the concept of the registration card scheme. She had been warned off this by people whose advice she normally relied on: the Police Federation, the Association of Chief Police Officers, magistrates

COMMONWEALTH GAMES THE TOP 15		
	Medals	
	G	S	B
Australia	52	54	56
England	47	40	42
Canada	35	41	36
New Zealand	17	14	27
India	13	8	11
Wales	10	3	12
Kenya	6	9	3
Nigeria	5	13	7
Scotland	5	7	10
Malaysia	2	2	-
Jamaica	2	-	2
Uganda	2	-	2
N. Ireland	1	3	5
Nauru	1	2	-
Hong Kong	1	1	3

and even her most loyal ally, the then environment secretary Nicholas Ridley. But it was not these who finally applied the *coup de grâce* but Lord Justice Taylor. His report on the Hillsborough disaster, which came out at the end of January, rejected the idea out of hand. He saw it as wholly irrelevant to the problem of containing hooliganism and indeed stated of the inveterate trouble-makers, 'They will see it as a challenge. Wrecking or circumventing it will add piquancy to the perverse pleasure they derive from their activities.'

With internal rows on Hong Kong, the poll tax and the prevailing ambulance strike all producing a clear impression of government instability, it did not seem likely that the government would keep on board a proposal on plastic cards and dubious technology which even the strong Thatcherite James Pawsey, MP for Rugby, described as 'crackers'. The bill was put to rest at the end of January.

But football was not to be let off the political hook so easily. The World Cup was to be considered the litmus test of the English spectators' behaviour and the future of both international and club football abroad would be determined by its success or failure. In the weeks leading up to the start of the finals the sports minister Colin Moynihan became a mini-General Haig, indulging in shuttle diplomacy as he winged tirelessly between London, Sardinia and Geneva, ensuring that nobody doubted the resolve of the government to take the most serious view of any misbehaviour and checking that the Italian authorities realised that it was as well for them to be prepared for a return jaunt of the Visigoths.

On an island which at times resembled an armed camp, the group in which England found themselves produced football of an indifferent nature. Scotland duly fell at the first hurdle as everybody including their own supporters had anticipated and England and the Republic of Ireland moved into the more meaningful second phase satisfied that the World Cup had not produced the mayhem which many had feared.

What then followed was least expected. The Republic of Ireland went to a dramatic and victorious penalty shoot-out against Romania, gained an audience with the Pope, led by Ireland's most famous Protestant and cigar-smoker, Jack Charlton, and took the hosts Italy all the way – only to be beaten by a single goal. That goal was scored by one of the unexpected heroes of the tournament, Salvatore Schillaci, whose sense of adventure and wild-eyed conviction could easily see him cast by Sergio Leone in a spaghetti western.

'I would like to thank Colin Moynihan and those who are higher than him. Most of us are.'
Brian Clough on the scrapping of football identity cards

Italy's consolation – Salvatore Schillaci's goal-scoring was one of the host country's few bright spots in the World Cup.

Bobby Robson, without whom the back pages – and sometimes the front – of the tabloids might have seemed uncommonly drab over the previous year, then found redemption as the English footballers, much like their compatriots in the Caribbean during the winter, suddenly discovered a spirit that had lain dormant for years. For there had been little doubt beforehand that England were well-enough endowed with talent. The problem for several decades had been in realising it properly and on cue. Against Belgium in extra time the substitute David Platt scored a goal of distinction. It was laid on by a young man of whom an entire English nation was now pleasantly conscious. Paul Gascoigne was now definitely 'Gazza'. He did not look the complete athlete but his brilliant, quirky style led England away from the chronic tunnel vision from which they seemed to have suffered too long and his talent was the equal of anyone in the tournament. Nevertheless, against the marvellously entertaining Cameroons, who were led by 38-year-old Roger Milla with such flair as to conjure up images of how Brazil had burst upon the world in Stockholm in 1958, England were fortunate to survive.

Watching the semi-final against West Germany, people, depending on their nationality, were either traumatised or transported by the penalty shoot-out. Parker's deflection had put the Germans in the lead but Lineker equalised. In the most vital penalty of all, after extra time, Stuart Pearce hit a flabby drive over the bar. The West Germans went through to win the cup in a squalid and easily forgettable encounter with Argentina. If the ending was sad the occasion was none the less something of a triumph for the style and attitude of the English players who had confounded their critics and were to go on to win FIFA's fair play award.

But the image indelibly stamped on the mind's eye was of Gazza who, having been booked by the referee in the semi-final and knowing that whatever the outcome of the game he would now be unable to play in the final, broke down and wept. As he tried to stem the tears with the tail of his jersey he suddenly lowered the mask from modern football's commercial and cynical face to reveal a little boy lost at the fair. Gascoigne came home to be fêted and for people to wonder how long his fresh personality could survive his burgeoning business interests and commercial exploitation. Although he seemed fated to become a millionaire it was equally apparent that nobody yet would begrudge him his reward.

'One of the great things about our match with the Germans was the lack of petulance or feigning of injury. If anyone lay down it was because they were hurt. The teams respected each other.'
Bobby Robson after England's defeat in the semi-finals of the World Cup

Gazza and Goochie. Sport's fondness for sobriquets could not have linked two who sounded more like a fading vaudeville duo but whose vitality had contributed to the longest continuum of pleasure for the English in sport for generations. From winter through to the tail-end of summer these two had suffered defeat, enjoyed victory but had combined to put a smile on the face of a nation which had looked at so much cricket and football in the past with no other option than to scowl.

In Britain, football enjoyed a successful year. Gates were up – even before the enthusiasm generated by the World Cup had an effect – and arrests were down. Liverpool and Rangers duly won their league championships, with Manchester United and Aberdeen winning the English and Scottish FA Cups. For the first time since the Heysel tragedy clubs from the football league – Aston Villa and Manchester United – were admitted to European club competitions. But optimism in football always needs to be tempered by realities of life. Swindon Town were promoted to the first division, but had to stay in the second division after the football authorities found that they had breached financial regulations. And in September tragedy struck at York City, when in a fourth division game their striker, David Longhurst, died due to a heart condition. He was the first player to die while playing in a football league game since 1927.

Rugby remained clean and wholesome. But neither was it easily predictable. In Edinburgh on 17 March the grand slam was at stake. The dashing and talented English were hot favourites to win. They ran out on to the pitch at Murrayfield to be greeted by as big a throng of their countrymen as had ever begged, borrowed or stolen tickets to gain entry. Then a strange thing happened. David Sole, the Scottish captain, chose to lead his men out on to the pitch with the measured pace of men walking in solemn procession towards some invocation of the gods. It had the effect of lifting the occasion from sporting contest to an examination of national psyche. It revealed a brooding and menacing Scottish belief in the territorial imperative and an intention of not surrendering an inch of soil. The emotional singing made 'Flower of Scotland' seem more hymn than anthem. They were staring the English in the eye and what they got in response was an averted glance. Scotland, playing their rugby the way they had entered the arena, possessed a voracious conviction the English could not match. After the initial Scottish onslaught, the English did effect a comeback of sorts but it was far from enough. The normally staid Scottish capital gave itself over to boisterous celebrations and one significant improvised banner summarised the afternoon by putting the scoreline into perspective: 'Bannockburn 1314, Murrayfield 13–7'.

If this had produced unexpected tremors they were but mild vibrations compared with the shock to the system most people experienced when they heard that someone named James 'Buster' Douglas had stopped Mike Tyson in the tenth round of their contest in February in the Tokyo Dome. Tyson was supposed to last as world champion until planet Earth fell into the

The day the earth moved . . . James 'Buster' Douglas knocks out Mike Tyson and becomes world heavyweight champion.

sun. But this result was greeted with universal relief by those who love boxing but were becoming distinctly testy at having to pay small fortunes to watch his fights. They were lucky if they lasted more than a couple of rounds and that was when Tyson had one of his bad nights.

Tyson's manager, an ex-prisoner called Don King, blamed the referee for a bad count and demanded that the boxing authorities strip the new man of his title. He was ignored. But it was difficult to ignore the fact that with golden oldies like Sugar Ray Leonard and Roberto Duran coining in millions for the geriatric confrontation of the year, boxing was ideally suited to Las Vegas and would survive in the future as an offshoot of nightclub cabaret.

Geriatric is not a phrase well-suited to a Wimbledon champion but compared with some now in the world game like fourteen-year-old Jennifer Capriati, Martina Navratilova is a dowager duchess. Without a tiara she mopped up the threat of Zena Garrison in the ladies' singles final to achieve a record-breaking ninth championship win. She still plays with an aggressive, almost superior, air and without much emotion, which is perhaps one of the qualities which lends a champion staying power.

Such is the thought that spectators might have formed watching Nick Faldo's year. His impassive, almost stern, approach to courses indicates a man who

Nick Faldo winning the US Masters in April. He went on to win the British Open in July.

seems to have programmed himself impeccably to a
specific system of action. None of the swashbuckling
cavalier approach of a Ballesteros for him. Faldo
advances on life with a measuring tape which, as a result
of 1990, he could well afford to have made of pure gold.
He retained his Masters title in Augusta, Georgia, in
April and tamed St Andrew's with an astonishing aggre-
gate score of 270 that had only been bettered in the past
by Tom Watson and Jack Nicklaus. His final round of
the Open in July was an example of his consummate
professionalism. He scorned treating the crowd to a
pyrotechnical finale and in taking his five at the notori-

**The man with
the golden
javelin - world
record holder
Steve Backley
winning gold at
the European
athletics
championships.**

ous Road Hole he seemed to eschew the challenge that
lay there like a man wisely skirting a minefield and
opted instead to create the atmosphere which suits his
clinical attitude well – anti-climax.

With much of Faldo's tall and commanding presence Steve Backley has become the man with the golden
arm. He became the first Briton ever to hold the world
record for the javelin throw. The man from Kent sent
the missile on its furthest journey ever on 2 July in
Stockholm, lost it again to Zelezny twelve days later and
regained it at Crystal Palace on 22 July with the first
throw ever over 90 metres. He exceeded it by .98 and
went on to win gold in the European Athletics Championships. He was truly Britain's athlete of the year.

The European Athletics Championships were
held in Split, Yugoslavia, at the end of August and

beginning of September. They helped confirm a massive enthusiasm for athletics. British fans were rewarded by an outstanding team performance – more medals than ever before at the championships.

There were many notable performances, including John Regis and Linford Christie, but the greatest popular interest was created by Peter Elliott. He had taken over the mantle of British middle-distance running from Coe, Ovett and the injured Cram and hopes were high for him in the 1,500 metres. It turned out to be a dramatic event, but for the wrong reasons. The fields in these events are increasing so much that the track sometimes looks like the M25 during the rush hour and accidents are occurring more often. In his semi-final Elliott was pushed off the course and out of the race by Hauke Fuhlbrugge of East Germany. Fuhlbrugge was disqualified, which was not surprising, but what was a surprise was that Elliott was allowed to compete in the final. Even some of his most ardent supporters were concerned at the precedent that this set. Perhaps inevitably, the final was a British anti-climax, with Elliott and Cram losing a last lap lead and finishing outside the medal positions.

The conflicting emotions experienced through the year might well have been neatly condensed in that single moment at Cheltenham when the nation's favourite, Desert Orchid, had to make way for a total unknown in the Gold Cup. As Dessie finished third, 100–1 Norton's Coin – regarded by his owner before the race as 'just a good handicapper' – raced to victory. The winner had earlier finished 40 lengths behind Dessie in the King George at Kempton. The elation of the Welsh owner stood out against the almost numb sadness of the majority at Cheltenham.

But the greatest finisher of all was Peter Blake. At 5.23 pm on 22 May he steered Steinlager over the winning line at Southampton as the clear winner of the Whitbread round the world yacht race. He had not only circumnavigated the world in just over 128 days, leaving a trail of contenders including the first all-women crew strung out behind, but also garlanded the globe with a ferocious courage and sense of purpose that reminded us that even in the year 1990 the greatest of all the sporting challenges are those which are natural and eternal.

FACING *the* FUTURE

Tackling – not just talking about – the

world's environmental problems will be a

crucial concern of the 1990s. So, too, will be

the search for an Aids cure to prevent the

projected deaths of 3 million women and children

Peter Sissons

S o, where do we go from here?
All I can venture is a summary of a number of basic themes, which I believe will dictate the quality of life and the progress of our country and the rest of mankind over the next few years. It is a personal view, written neither from boardroom, workshop, laboratory or legislature. It is the view from where I sit in the newsroom.

The international framework in prospect was spelled out by Mikhail Gorbachev at the beginning of September after his meeting in Helsinki with George Bush: 'No single country, however powerful, will be able to provide the leadership which individual countries formerly tried to provide, including some countries which are represented here.' Hopes are running high of a new world order. The disintegration of the Soviet bloc, and with it the last relics of Marxist ambition, expansionism and spheres of ideological domination, unlocked years of tedious and dangerous ritual confrontation. And the hopes for the future received their most important boost from the unprecedented unanimity of the United Nations Security Council in its series of votes on the Iraqi invasion of Kuwait.

Suddenly, the term 'international law' has taken

on a new stature. And the obverse of that old coin with a new shine is that the term 'international outlaw' may also take on a new significance. The world, however, will need leadership of fine judgment and high quality to make these hopes a reality. Mr Gorbachev appears acutely conscious that, at the outset, the necessary qualification for leadership will not be vision, determination or the ownership of a nuclear arsenal. Leadership is going to be bound up as never before with economic power. At Helsinki, it was a sensitive topic for the Soviets, prompting a vigorous denial by Mr Gorbachev that he was following the US lead in the Gulf crisis to secure economic aid: 'It would be very oversimplified and very superficial to judge that the Soviet Union could be bought for dollars.'

However, there is an ironic sub-text that will run through the question of world leadership, which, as we have seen, did not escape Gorbachev. In the very hour that the United States stands triumphant in the victory of capitalism, so it, too, has to confess that America no longer has the economic strength to put its hegemony beyond question. The pleas that the United States has made to the world's richest economies – Germany and Japan – to share the costs of the crusade against Saddam Hussein tell their own story. If Saddam Hussein is brought down by sanctions and not shells, we may yet be able to say the yen is mightier than the sword.

But the prospects for the Soviet Union, as it struggles with the onset of perestroika's bleakest winter, is the great unknown. Mr Gorbachev changed the world, but he cannot put sausages on the shelves of supermarkets. He has thousands of Soviet troops in Germany who cannot come home because he cannot afford to feed and house them without German help. The Soviet leader himself is more respected abroad than at home. So will the man who changed the world be swept away because he cannot manage the changes he has unleashed in his own country?

The next few months may tell us the answers. For now, the distinguished Moscow correspondent of *The Independent* newspaper, Rupert Cornwell, has this stark assessment: 'Never has daily Soviet life seemed more brutalised by failure and shortage . . . there is the tangible feeling that something terrible is in the air.' And *The Times*, in an eloquent leader bearing the hallmark of its new editor, Simon Jenkins, puts it this way: 'The question is whether the heirs of Lenin, who exterminated the commercial classes after 1917, and of Stalin, who annihilated the independent farmers and most of the intelligentsia, should now be entrusted with the

IMAGES *of* 1990

Anti-poll tax
protester hurls
chair at
mounted police
outside the
National
Gallery in
London.

resurrection of capitalism in the Soviet empire . . . Mr Gorbachev must soon have to choose between his past ideological allegiance and his present office . . . Winter looms and bread is short: it is time for all good men to leave the party.' The Soviet Union may change even faster than anyone could have predicted.

The end of 1990 will almost certainly be the beginning of the time when the industrialised world will have to start making some stern choices about the environment. If the 1980s were the decade of environmental concern, the 1990s must be the years of action. But some of the omens are not good. Parts of Eastern Europe are a poisoned industrial wasteland. Managing the trick of cleaning them up and curing their capacity to inflict chronic illness, while putting more modern technology in their place, and avoiding mass unemployment and the political instability that goes with it, will test political, technical and management skills to their limits.

The task is almost certainly much greater and more costly than first envisaged. For instance, the West German environment minister warned in September that after reunification, East Germany's Soviet-made nuclear power plants – there are five and six more are under construction – may have to be closed for good because it would cost too much to make them safe. He said this in the knowledge that decommissioning a nuclear power station is a dauntingly expensive operation in itself.

Elsewhere, tackling the wider, global problems of ozone depletion and the greenhouse effect may pose fundamental dilemmas for the industrialised world. What if the scientists – or at least those the politicians feel compelled to believe – prescribe measures to save the planet that need really radical changes in lifestyles and social and industrial practice? How easy will it be to introduce such measures within any democratic political framework – of the new order or of the old? Will politicians introduce necessary measures which may lose them the next election? Can such profound change as is judged necessary to save our environment be introduced within countries obsessed with the election cycle?

The omens from the political response to past imperatives in energy policy are not good. As Anatole Kaletsky wrote in *The Financial Times* about the Gulf crisis: '. . . the third Middle Eastern oil shock brings to mind the dictum that history repeats itself first as tragedy and then as farce. The West's military and political strategy has been brilliantly handled; but the

'Provided others are ready to take their full share, Britain is prepared to set itself the very demanding target of a reduction of up to 30% in presently projected levels of carbon dioxide emissions by the year 2005.'
Mrs Thatcher at the opening of a new research centre into climatic change

---

'The rhetoric was right, the action recommended was totally wrong. We need deep cuts in carbon dioxide emissions now.'
Dr Jeremy Leggett, Greenpeace

guardians of energy policy in Europe, Japan and America have acted with the strategic vision of the Keystone Cops. As the scientists begin to bring in the fruits of the definitive studies ordered from them about what has to be done to protect the planet, can we rely on there being the political will to implement them?'

A British environment minister, David Trippier, promised at a UN environment conference in Norway in May that Britain's national strategy to control greenhouse gases, 'will have serious implications for transport and energy'. And he warned of 'pain and anguish' in the battle to curb rising emissions from traffic and industry. The same month, Mrs Thatcher, who was honoured by the United Nations with an award for outstanding environmental achievement, called for a 'giant international effort' to save the earth from the consequences of global warming, but disappointed many environmentalists by pledging only to stabilise UK emissions at the present levels by 2005, and only if other nations did their share. One of the more restrained adverse reactions to that came from the chief executive of the Meteorological Office, who thought the Thatcher proposals merely bought time.

The gap between what the scientists judge necessary, and what the politicians contemplate may prove very, very difficult to bridge in the next crucial period of decision. Set next to the prime minister's target, the Intergovernmental Panel on Climate Change, predicting that by the middle of the next century temperatures will be $3°C$ higher than at present, believes that ultimately an 80 per cent reduction will be necessary to stabilise the levels of greenhouse gases. But at the economic summit at Houston in July, President Bush made it plain that he regarded any permanent limits on such emissions as an unacceptable restriction on America's economic growth.

Meanwhile, it is possible that the entire debate may be re-opened by scientists who believe the whole preoccupation with global atmospherics is ill founded. The holders of such views draw on historical evidence of natural climatic variations. If there were once vineyards in Edinburgh, why shouldn't changes in our weather make viniculture in Scotland possible again? Dr Roy Spencer, a physicist at the Nasa Marshall Space Flight Centre, told Channel 4's *Equinox* programme on 12 August: 'It's easier to get funding if you can show some evidence for impending climate disasters. In the late 1970s it was the coming ice age and now it's global warming. Who knows what it will be ten years from now? Sure, science benefits from scary scenarios.' It

On Friday, 3 August, a temperature of 98.8°F, 37.1°C, was recorded in a garden in Cheltenham, making it Britain's hottest day since records began.

IMAGES *of* 1990

Two workmen were killed near Petersfield as violent storms caused damage in January.

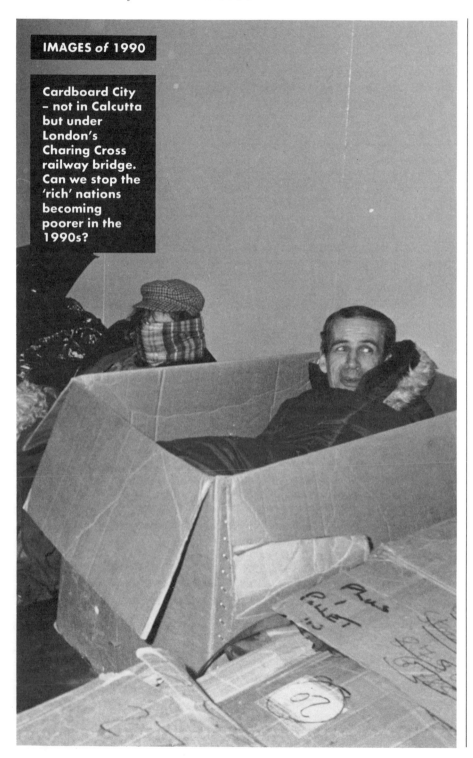

IMAGES *of* 1990

Cardboard City – not in Calcutta but under London's Charing Cross railway bridge. Can we stop the 'rich' nations becoming poorer in the 1990s?

would save everyone a lot of trouble if Dr Spencer were right. But what sort of a risk would it be if the world simply waits to find out?

Not prepared to wait, but for other reasons, will be many countries in the third world. Alongside their expanding populations goes growing demand for consumables such as cheap refrigerators and cars. And where they have their own capacity to produce goods, the chemicals and processes they use are often the very polluters that the rich nations are trying to abolish. Why should they forgo raising their meagre living standards because politicians in the rich countries say they must play their part in protecting the planet? Since the debate over global warming got into its stride, the poor nations have been telling the rest of the world that if it wants them to forgo certain industrial processes or take expensive steps to curb pollution, the rich nations will have to pay.

Nineteen ninety did bring some progress, with India and China, who account for a third of mankind, accepting that CFCs must be phased out. But one can say for certain that, after the new impetus towards international awareness and co-operation in 1990, international relations between North and South will be made vastly more complicated by the quest for new environmental treaties. Does anyone have the faintest idea of how to square the circle of an increasing third world population – feeding it, meeting its material ambitions, and getting it to promise that it won't make a nasty environmental mess like the developed world has? Here is an illustration of the scale of the problem: Pope John Paul first visited Africa in 1980. There were then 55 million Catholics in his African flock. When he returned in 1990, there were 79 million. Overall, on present trends, Africa's population of 550 million will grow to 1.6 billion in the next thirty years. Catastrophic economic decline is forecast unless something is done. But the Pope returned to Rome having repeated his implacable opposition to artificial methods of birth control.

In health organisations and ministries throughout the world, there is deep concern about Aids. It is possible that the true extent of the concern is sometimes suppressed – for political reasons, and to avoid scaremongering. As a journalist, I have an uneasy feeling that, as we begin the short haul to the millennium, Aids is going to be seen as a much more serious threat than hitherto. On the same African tour in 1990, the Pope made clear that he also opposed safe sex programmes that advocated the use of condoms. He

IMAGES *of* 1990

Strangeways Prison siege ends with clenched fist act of defiance after twenty-five days.

IMAGES *of* 1990

Free at last – US hostage Frank Reed, released after forty-three months' captivity in Lebanon.

believed, he told the faithful in the Tanzanian capital, Dar es Salaam, that such programmes actually encouraged the sort of behaviour that spreads Aids. Field workers were dismayed. The World Health Organisation, in a report published at the end of July, forecast that at least three million women and children will die from Aids in this decade, and that several million un-infected children will be orphaned when their parents die from Aids. The report, published in *The Lancet*, was a remorseless catalogue of the prospects for mass human misery. It stated that for young women aged between twenty and forty in big US cities, Western Europe and sub-Saharan Africa, Aids is now the leading cause of death. By early this year, three million women, 80 per cent of them in sub-Saharan Africa, had become infected with HIV. By 1992, four million children worldwide will be born to HIV-infected women, a quarter of them affected in the womb. The report declared: 'The social, economic, and demographic impacts on women and children have been largely neglected.' It records, 'a slow but steady increase in HIV infections among the heterosexual population,' and notices a marked increase in infant and child mortality – in some areas, of as much as 30 per cent. The figures would be bad for a disease that is curable. The stark prospect for the Nineties is that Aids may be no more curable than the common cold is curable. But it takes only days to incubate the common cold. Aids is an incurable disease with an incubation period of up to ten years, which, if it advances at the present rate, could become the great plague of the twenty-first century. Man has never needed science more.

During the last months of 1990, as the world waited to see if war would start in the Gulf, television took another stride forward – not just as a window, but as a catalyst for international events. The speed with which the regime in Baghdad and the administration in Washington were able to trade insult, admonition, threat and other propaganda became a matter for some concern. As the electronic task force from Ted Turner's Cable News Network flashed, live, the latest developments from one capital to the other, voices were raised questioning this latest advance in the relationship between television and conflict. Western television was accused of being Iraq's greatest asset, giving the dictator access to western living rooms, without corresponding privileges in the other direction.

It was an inevitable step for television, and the evidence is that CNN acquitted itself well. But the development placed new responsibilities on journalists, who had never before been tested to such an extent by the constant tendency of the speed of the medium to outstrip the procedures of sound editorial judgment. However, in such a situation, it could be possible that the best safeguard would be a number of genuine international, twenty-four-hour, television news providers, in the CNN mould. Such a thought may revive speculation about the possible international impact of a satellite television arm of the BBC World Service. But the costs, as Ted Turner testifies, have made strong men wince.

The return on such costs will not, however, be measured on any conventional balance sheet. Despite the advances for democracy in Eastern Europe, it is impossible to quantify whether the world is becoming a more or less democratic place as a whole. The group of seven, at their Houston summit in July 1990, confidently declared that the 1990s will be the 'decade of democracy', and reiterated their commitment to strengthening democracy and human rights worldwide. How is the momentum to be kept up? Amnesty International is one organisation which is certain that one of the most positive developments is the way in which communications technology and the international media are allowing people to see much more of what is happening in the world. The Nineties could be the decade in which television, about whose future it is easy to be sceptical, opens millions more eyes to the possibilities as well as the horrors of the human condition. And in opening those eyes to a Tiananmen Square or a Berlin Wall, we now know that changes which in the past took decades are now capable of being precipitated within weeks. It is the lesson of the immediate past, and the daunting prospect before us.

Who DIED *in* 1990

Allen Adams 44, Labour MP. Mel Appleby 22, singer in pop group *Mel and Kim.* Leonard Bernstein 72, composer. Dr Bruno Bettelheim 86, American psychologist. Lord Caradon 86, former colonial governor. Michael Carr 43, Labour MP. Robert Carvel 71, journalist. Ian Charleson 40, actor. Sammy Davis Jr 64, entertainer. John Evans 112, oldest man in Britain. Bernard Falk 47, journalist and broadcaster. Greta Garbo 84, actress. Lord Gardiner 89, former Lord Chancellor. Ava Gardner 67, actress. Lord Bruce-Gardyne 60, former treasury minister. Ian Gow 53, Conservative MP. Jane Grigson 61, cookery writer. Lord Cecil Harmsworth 87, publisher and painter. Sir Rex Harrison 82, actor. Jim Henson 53, creator of *The Muppets.* Robert Holmes à Court 53, Australian entrepreneur. Sean Hughes 44, Labour MP. Sir Len Hutton 74, cricketer. Jill Ireland 53, actress. Gordon Jackson 66, actor. Peter Jones 60, BBC sports commentator. Bill Keys 67, trade unionist. Bruno Kriesky 79, former Austrian chancellor. Margaret Lockwood 73, actress. Joe Loss 80, bandleader. Harold McCusker 50, Unionist MP. Joe Mercer 76, footballer. Colin Milburn 48, cricketer. Richard Murdoch 83, radio comedian. Cardinal Tomas O Fiaich 66, Archbishop of Armagh and Primate of all Ireland. Lord O'Neill of the Maine 75, former prime minister, Northern Ireland. Norman Parkinson 76, photographer. Michael Powell 84, film director. Bhagwan Shree Rajneesh 58, Indian guru. Johnnie Ray 63, singer. Major Pat Reid 79, Colditz escaper. Allan Roberts 46, Labour MP. Lord (Victor) Rothschild 79, scientist and civil servant. Leonard Sachs 80, MC on BBC's *The Good Old Days.* Alberto Semprini 81, pianist. Del Shannon 50, 1960s pop singer. Barbara Stanwyck 82, actress. Lord Stewart of Fulham 83, former foreign secretary. Lord Swann 70, former BBC chairman. A. J. P. Taylor 84, historian. Le Duc Tho 79, Vietnamese communist leader. Terry-Thomas 78, actor. Mandy Turner 21, cancer campaigner. Sarah Vaughan 66, jazz singer. Max Wall 82, comedian. Pat Wall 57, Labour MP.

Picture credits